The Perfect Nonprofit Model

The Perfect Nonprofit

A Holistic, Balanced Approach to Nonprofit Management

David F. Condon & Kevin W. Bingham

Diversified Nonprofit Services

Printing history: May 2009: First Edition

Library of Congress Cataloging-in-Publication Data

Condon, David

The Perfect Nonprofit: A Holistic, Balanced Approach to Nonprofit Management /
David F. Condon and Kevin W. Bingham

LCCN: 2009924453

ISBN-13: 978-0-615-28363-0

Book layout and design: Edzard de Ranitz & Ewart Newton

Contents

Prologue: It All Begins Here! vii

Introduction x

Chapter 1: What is The Perfect Nonprofit? 1

Chapter 2: Mission and Vision - Our Reason for Being 6

Your Mission Must Live Within Your Heart....................................6

Strategy Development..7

Does Your Organization Have Vision?...10

Vision Is About More Than Growth..12

A Final Thought..13

Chapter 3: Professional Leadership - the Art of Leading from Behind...15

Core Tasks of the Agency Executive...16

Effectively Manage the Day-to-Day Operations of
Your Organization..17

Create Synergy with the Board 18

Assure Financial Transparency and Viability 19

Implement Organizational Goals and Objectives...................20

Assure Effective Governance..21

Know Your Customer..22

The Perfect Nonprofit Executive...25

Exhibit Humility...26

Create Organizational Synergy 26

Focus on the Important...26

Ensure Balance...26

Find Value in Everyone 27

Chapter 4: Resource Development and Marketing
- Where the Rubber Meets the Road 28

Resource Development...*28*

Human Resources and Leadership Development.........................30

Mission-Driven Planning for Resource Development.................33

It's All About the Investors: Investor Identification, Cultivation,
Recruitment, Acknowledgement, and Retention 35

It Takes a Village: Community Collaboration..............................43

Resource Development: The Tangible vs. the
Intangible for Your Organization..45

The Importance of the Internal Resource Development Audit.............46

Marketing as a Vital Tool in Resource Development *48*

Nontraditional Forms of Marketing Available
to All Nonprofit Organizations...51

The Final Test: Raising Money in Challenging Times 57

Keys to Raising Money in Times of Change 57

Chapter 5: Board Leadership - the Inexact Science 61

The Three Types of Board Leadership *61*

Inverted Model...62

Micro-Management Model 62

Balanced Model..63

Eight Key Functions of the Board..64

Advocate! Advocate! Advocate! 67

Engage at a High Level..68

Persevere Through the Good, the Bad and the Ugly 70

Strategize for the Future 71

Be Accountable to Yourself and Others................................73

Garner Resources in a Zealous Fashion................................74

Set Governance Structure that Builds Public Trust.............75

Provide Leadership and Insight..76

Chapter 6: Governance - the Foundation of Achievement......81

Developing the TEAM That Will Carry You to Success.................82

A Different Governance Model for Different Times.......................83

Understanding Nonprofit Finance...87

The Nonprofit Paradigm 87

Understanding the Expense Side 91

Legal Duties of the Board and Organization..............................92

Conclusion..94

Chapter 7: Quality and Impactful Services to Clients
- Begin with the End..95

Service Delivery...95

Community Assessment...95

Identifying the Need 95

Identification of Key Leadership and Philanthropic Centers 97

Collaboration and Partnership 97

Using the Results 98

Defining Your Impact *99*

Communicating Your Impact *102*

Description of Service Delivery Models *103*

Summary *107*

Chapter 8: Diagnostic - Measuring your Perfection Quotient 109

Perfection Quotient Quality Statements *112*

Mission and Vision 112

Professional Leadership 114

Resource Development and Marketing 118

Board Leadership 122

Governance 125

High Quality and Impactful Services to Clients 129

Chapter 9: Perfect Practice Makes Perfect 132

Getting Started *134*

Glossary **135**

Prologue: It All Begins Here!

Somewhere in the formative stages of every nonprofit agency, people come together to create an organization with a central focus of helping people, animals, the environment, or any number of other laudable causes. If they achieve their goal, there is little doubt in their minds that their efforts will improve the quality of life for mankind. Their boundless energy coupled with a desire to help society in some way leads to the formation and certification of a nonprofit agency. In most cases, the desire to help becomes the central focus. Exactly how this is going to be accomplished is quite often put on the backburner. Little thought is given to the infrastructure needed for a sound organization, the funding required to make it viable, the leadership necessary to carry it out, the scope of the vision and mission to be the backbone of the organization, and last but not least, the proof of the need for the organization in the first place.

"The Perfect Game" is the blending of dedication, practice, training, knowledge, vision, teamwork, and yes, even some luck. In order for a Perfect Game to occur, all of these components, while following different paths, timelines and schedules, will intersect and meld into one shining moment of glory that becomes The Perfect Game. Should one of these components be eliminated, altered, or take a different path, or if the timing is off by even a fraction of a minute, The Perfect Game will be just another afternoon at the ballpark.

Eventually, these things bond into one game-changing the event and a nonprofit organization is born. However, unlike the Perfect Game scenario, the result is rarely perfection. In most cases, the result is chaos and fragmentation where one component of the nonprofit takes precedence over all others, thus limiting the chances for not only perfection, but for success. There is little doubt that while their causes are great and the desire to help is genuine, the planning of each facet of the organization is not given equal weight and attention. Often, there is no balance in the process so the organization struggles or never reaches its full potential.

The Perfect Nonprofit Model is a holistic approach to moving your organization towards becoming the type of nonprofit you may only have dreamed of at the start, by bringing together all of the components that must be integrated into creating perfection within your organization. *The Perfect Nonprofit* Model will show you how to integrate leadership, governance, marketing, strategic thinking, and resource development while moving your organization towards perfection. It has been said, "Real perfection is in the striving to be perfect that leads you to set new goals and objectives which just keeps it out of reach."

Together, Kevin Bingham and David Condon have forty-five years of nonprofit management experience. They own and operate Diversified Nonprofit Services, a nationally recognized company with over twenty-four years of experience in nonprofit consulting. Nonprofit organizations have raised almost one billion dollars throughout the United States using Diversified Nonprofit Services models and services. Kevin and David have used this vast experience along with the collective thinking of their staff, professional relationships developed over many years, and research conducted to develop this approach to nonprofit management.

Learning and implementing *The Perfect Nonprofit* Model will lead your organization to a balanced management process while utilizing practices and principles applied in the most successful businesses and nonprofit organizations in America. Implementing this process and these principles will undoubtedly help you to guide your organization beyond what you ever envisioned. *The Perfect Nonprofit* will prepare you to take the field for your "Perfect Game." You will continually be able to set new goals and objectives that, while moving your organization forward, will keep total perfection just out of reach. By doing this your organization will become *The Perfect*

Nonprofit.

Further information, tools, and services are available at
www.theperfectnonprofit.com

Dedication

Writing this book has been a love of ours, while also requiring
an enormous amount of effort and patience from others. We'd
like to dedicate this book to our loving wives Connie and Laurie
who spent countless hours reading and rereading this book,
and for allowing us the time to spend away from them and
our families to compile our knowledge and experience from
which this book is derived. We'd also like to thank our team
at Diversified Nonprofit Services who have been incredibly
positive and encouraging through this process.

Enjoy The Perfect Nonprofit!!!

David F. Condon & Kevin W. Bingham

Introduction

In the nonprofit world, everyone seems to be looking for that silver bullet that overcomes a problem that keeps them from performing the job they are charged with doing. For example, "I know what we can do; we'll just hire a grant writer to raise the money we need to operate." If you have sat in as many boardrooms as I have, this statement will drive you crazy. Nonprofit boards all across this country sit in monthly meetings and focus on issues that are of little or no importance to their overall well-being. Now do not close this book if this statement offends you. You may be leading or serving on a board that is focusing on only their well-being. If you are, then you are in the minority. In addition, many nonprofits operate out of the bounds of the constitution and by-laws originally comprised to form the organization. I would contend that at least 40 percent of the meetings conducted by nonprofit organizations are not even legal meetings. Most meetings do not meet the quorum requirements laid out in the organization's by-laws while others do not qualify because insufficient notice was given prior to the meeting. I have actually sat through board meetings in which not only were there no minutes of the previous meeting, but there was no previous profit-and-loss statement given. Can you imagine governing an organization and not knowing the financial standing of it? Sadly, this happens often in the nonprofit sector.

While boards are governing by the seats of their pants and decisions affecting the organization are being made in illegal meetings, the executive is standing at the helm guiding the organization through the fog. Or are they? The position we refer to as the executive professional is ever shifting to meet the changing landscape of the nonprofit organization. Many executive professionals rule with a strong hand and dictate the activities of the board and the organization, while others are simply program people who have been promoted beyond their ability to perform. Although the majority of nonprofit executive professionals fall somewhere between these two places in the spectrum, it is essential that executive professionals be at the top of their game to be successful.

Of course, very few nonprofits go very far without having to confront the one word that sends board members and professionals alike running for the hills. This word is *funding*. The areas of Resource Development and Marketing are essential to the success of any nonprofit. Many nonprofit boards have this pure, virtuous thought that if they work toward accomplishing their mission and vision, manna will fall from heaven in the form of money and all needs will be met. Although I would like to believe this, we live in a country whose economy is built on the almighty dollar, not good intentions. While it is important for nonprofits to meet the covenants of their mission, it is the job of those in charge to assure that adequate resources are in place to meet that need. Below is an example of how boards run away from this responsibility.

The Perfect Example: Scared to Death!

In my first job as an executive professional, the board and I were charged with opening a new organization. This was back in the day when growth was the calling card of the day in all nonprofits. I had a board of well-intending people and I had a board president who was tenacious. We rolled along pretty well for several months but then we began to run short on funds. It began to get quite serious. So being the "rookie," I asked the board president to bring this up at the next scheduled meeting of the board of directors and he did. He explained the shortfall in funds, and as the conversation continued, I noticed that people began to quietly get up and leave the meeting. Once the discussion was over, we went from having eleven board members present to having four in attendance. They all ran. It scared them to death!

I learned a valuable lesson that night, which will be covered in the chapter on Professional Leadership. The reason behind the story above is that boards and executive professionals have an innate fear of Resource Development and Marketing.

If all of the above does not paint an ugly enough picture, in the past several years, I have watched nonprofits walk away from their mission and vision. While I mentioned above that mission alone cannot drive an organization, it must be at the forefront of all decision-making endeavors.

Lastly, the nonprofit sector is very much into what I call the "flavor of the month." If someone has a crisis, everyone focuses solely on crisis management. If the executive professional is in flux, everyone focuses on this. I could go on and on and on. Those of you in the field know what I mean. If you are new to all of this, just read on. Trust me.

Now for what I believe is the best news the nonprofit sector has seen in years, we have developed a nonprofit management tool that actually makes sense. Yes, it really does. It applies common sense approaches and strategies to meet your everyday organizational needs. This model has been developed by professionals who have spent years sitting at the helm of nonprofit organizations and by others who have sat on the other side of the table as board volunteers. In addition, we have been privy to the services delivered by national nonprofits whose focus is to provide capacity-building services to their constituents. These experiences have allowed us to develop what we call

The Perfect Nonprofit.

We know that many, if not most of you, do not believe it is possible to be perfect in any way. As a matter of fact, I believe this myself. Except, what is wrong with striving to be perfect?

What is wrong with looking for a tool that will help you move your nonprofit in this direction? My response to this would be, "Nothing." As you read this book, remember that portions may seem somewhat elementary to you. If they do, show great attention and caution as you read these sections of the book, for many times what we feel is our greatest strength is also our greatest weakness. In closing, keep in mind that the greatest things ever invented in life were based on simplicity and common sense so let me be the first to welcome you to *The Perfect Nonprofit!*

What is *The Perfect Nonprofit?*

1

If you were running your own business and someone
approached you and said they could provide you with a map to
success, what would you do? Regrettably, in the world we live in
today, many people would laugh and throw this person out of
their office. A large part of my nonprofit experience was spent
working in field services for a national organization. I have to
say, it was one of the most rewarding jobs I ever held. In this
job, I had the opportunity to work with multiple nonprofit
member organizations in the same geographic area.

I once visited a local executive professional in the southern
and western parts of our nation. This young executive had
shown a propensity to be very successful. As I was visiting with
him one day, I was really patting him on the back about his
accomplishments. In the middle of my telling him how good
he was, he stopped me and said, "Your comments are really
nice and I really appreciate them but you do not understand
my world." As I looked at him in a questioning way, he went
on to say, "You see, we all operate by the Sand Crab Theory. If
you place several Sand Crabs in a bucket and watch them, one
will try and crawl out. If the crab gets close to climbing out, the
others will grab it and pull it back into the bucket."

This story is so profound to me. As I have made my way around
this nation and talked with other nonprofit leaders, it is my fear
that we all operate in this fashion. I make this point because
there will be those who turn their nose up at this model because
it is based on four simple but integral covenants:

- *The Perfect Nonprofit* Model is simple and easy to
  understand. This does not make it unsophisticated.

- *The Perfect Nonprofit* Model is holistic. The parts of
  the model must all work harmoniously for success.

- *The Perfect Nonprofit* Model is predicated in balance. Nonprofits must work toward balance and not fall for the "flavor of the month" philosophy.

- *The Perfect Nonprofit* Model is all about common sense. We will not fill you with jargon. The model does have some theory, but it is backed up with common sense thoughts to apply to assure the model works.

While the four covenants dictate how *The Perfect Nonprofit* operates, there are four key components that wrap around the mission and vision of any nonprofit. All of these result in high quality and impactful services to the client. The model is better visualized in the chart below followed by a more detailed description.

The Perfect Nonprofit Model

This model may look very elementary and simple; remember, this is our intent! As I mentioned earlier in the introduction, many businesses fail, be it for-profit or nonprofit, because they do not grasp the key components that add up to success in all organizations like them. Again, I know some of you out there are saying, "We do not need something like this to enhance or develop our organization; we are doing just fine." My experience would lead me to believe that you need this worse than the next guy.

We all have our heroes, the people that mold and shape our lives. You know, those people who you want to be like when you grow up. Typically we all have three or four of these people in our lives if we are lucky. My hero is my father. He was an educator first and a high school football coach second. One of the things he used to tell me in relation to anything I was doing was very simply, "If you aren't getting better, you are getting worse." I still believe this to this day. *The Perfect Nonprofit* Model will allow you and your organization to get better.

As you can see from the graph above, the four key components that comprise *The Perfect Nonprofit* Model are wrapped around the mission and vision. What makes the implementation, oversight and success of a nonprofit different from that of a for-profit business is the call to the mission and vision of the organization. If you truly adhere to the laws that govern nonprofits, you must have a mission statement that identifies and dictates the action of your organization. In my mind, this is a true covenant of nonprofit management. Your mission and vision must drive your organization; hence, the rotation of the Four Key Components around the Mission and Vision of the organization. Before any decision is made in reference to the Four Key Components, it must be measured against the Mission and Vision of the organization.

The importance of professional leadership to the success of any nonprofit is a key component to *The Perfect Nonprofit* Model. Every year, thousands of nonprofits are sanctioned by the Internal Revenue Service. Over half of these new nonprofits will hire an executive professional. The nonprofit sector is already in desperate need for quality leaders to run these businesses. Sadly, as in many nonprofits, potential leaders often work in small micro-nonprofits and never gain the expertise and experience to move up the ladder and eventually surface to run a major nonprofit. This experience is much the same in the public and private sectors. It comes down to this: there is a shortfall of leadership and talent needed to run nonprofits. This quandary poses many questions about Professional Leadership that we will cover in depth later in the book.

Boards, boards, boards! You gotta love 'em! Wow, what were our forefathers thinking when they came up with the requirement that every nonprofit have a governing board? My contention is that their forethought was right on the money. There is no other way to run a corporation. The bottom line with board development and leadership is that it is a science that must be worked on and perfected. The hiccup in this is that those people who are the supposed experts on board development and leadership spend more time talking about theory and what boards "should be doing" than they do on applying what I call "real world" application. Board leadership and development is a key cog in the success of any nonprofit and will also be discussed at length.

One thing that any nonprofit leader needs to understand is this: the fact you are a nonprofit organization does not mean that you have to be poor and living hand to mouth. As a matter of fact, it is a downright bad strategy to apply. In addition, being a nonprofit does not mean there is not a market share of wealth and education out there so you must grab your share of it. Resource Development and Marketing seem to be the most difficult concepts for boards and executives to grasp, but are the most important. Ironically, it is the easiest to remedy if you just apply some simple principles to your development and marketing efforts. Of course, you will not want to miss this cliffhanger of a chapter.

Lastly, but just as important as all others, Governance is the

1

final key component. It should be a very important cog in the wheel, but no more important and no more emphasized than any of the other key components. Governance is about how your organization behaves and how you communicate to your key stakeholders or constituents.

The end result of mastering the four key components, wrapped around the Mission and Vision of the organization, will be your customer client base being more than pleased with the service you are providing. It is our firm belief and passion that adherence to this model will yield a high customer satisfaction quotient for your organization. At the end of the day you will meet the Mission and Vision of your organization.

When this happens, you can declare victory and start the process over again! What a world!

Further information, tools, and services are available at www.theperfectnonprofit.com

Mission and Vision - Our Reason for Being

2

Your Mission Must Live Within Your Heart

A Mission Statement is a statement of the intrinsic beliefs of an organization that clearly states the organization's purpose, focus, service population, and desired outcome. The Mission Statement need not be long but should provide defined direction for the organization as it strives to meet the needs of its constituents.

Having briefly outlined what an organization's mission should be, it needs to be stated that the concept of the mission for many nonprofits is often the most misunderstood and misused explanation of what the central focus and essence of the organization is. In many cases, the mission of a local organization is adopted from the general Mission Statement of the national organization that they are affiliated with. Even more common is using words that someone in the organization thinks are meaningful in the execution of meeting the community's needs but once written are never revisited or graded against how well the organization is actually meeting those needs. In many years of nonprofit consulting, I cannot tell you how many organizations have never once revisited their original Mission Statement in relation to the type and focus of the services they are presently providing to their service population.

Your Mission Statement should be a living, breathing manifestation of what you do each and every day in your agency in meeting the needs of your service population; needs that have been verified, qualified, and certified through extensive testing and evaluation of the community. The statement is not something you print out on your agenda each month just to remind board members of what it says. It is not something you keep in a locked drawer to be reviewed at the annual meeting. Your Mission Statement must be carried in the heart of each and every employee, board member, and community volunteer that is part of your agency.

Strategy Development

The entire concept of developing a Mission Statement and/or reviewing one you already have for modification is a process of knowing the focus of your organization. Who are you dedicated to serving? How are these services going to be maximized to ensure the desired impact and outcomes? The perfect forum for this evaluation is part of a formal Strategy Development process that not only forces you to evaluate and either confirm or change your Mission Statement but also directs your board and staff in confirming what your Core Purpose is, what your Core Identity is, and what Core Values drive your organization toward operational and service excellence.

Note that I did not use the term *Strategic Planning*. The concept of the traditional Strategic Planning model creates a static plan with goals and objectives to be attained over a three- to five-year timeframe with the objective of transforming the agency over that period into a better functioning, more dynamic organization. The flaw in this model from my perspective is that there is no immediacy or urgency; the plan does not have specific Goals and Objectives assigned to specific board members and staff; and the timeframe is so long it does not allow for the rapidly changing dynamics in the world as we know it today. The Strategy Development process I refer to is a dynamic process that can be completed with a sound functioning board of directors over a period of thirty to forty-five hours with a full-day retreat as the focal point. This process takes the information developed in the organization's community assessment (see chapter of Service Delivery) and uses it to identify who, what, when, where, and why of the organization's central core. The process is designed on a model that seeks to transform the culture of a nonprofit organization from a nonprofit management model to a proactive business model, which essentially leads to the abandonment of the traditional donor/contributor philosophy to one that focuses the agency on an investor/return on investment philosophy.

The Strategy Development process is predicated on creating an interactive TEAM of staff, board, and community volunteers to identify no more than four to six key strategies that will be addressed in a period of twelve to eighteen months immediately following the retreat. Further, it establishes goals and objectives to address each of these strategies. This "alignment" assigns the responsibility for their execution to multidisciplinary teams made up of board, staff, and in some cases community volunteers.

The Strategy Development process forces the organization to confront the real issues facing it and to fine tune the way it thinks about board development, leadership, governance, resource development, marketing, mission, vision, and service delivery. The reader will note that each and every one of these components make up the structure of the holistic model we call

Mission and Vision -
Our Reason for Being

2

The Perfect Nonprofit. Moreover, it uses a monthly tracking system to ensure that each one is being addressed and is moving forward or can be altered in terms of assigned accountability and/or execution to ensure that no aspect of the process can derail the whole plan.

The comparison to the old fashioned static form Strategic Planning is limited to the word *Strategy* being a part of each process. However, the comparison ends there. The Strategy Development process as outlined here sets the stage for the creation of a proactive, dynamic organization that can respond to changes in the economic and/or social environment. Below is a diagram that outlines the process an organization proceeds through when completing a successful strategy development session. A real desire to change must exist for the organization to create a clear vision for the future, followed by a process that is aligned and engaging. Lastly, the organization must clearly have a desire to reach its envisioned future.

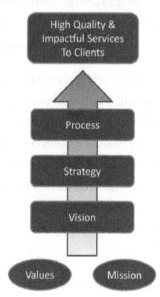

Strategy Model

Does Your Organization Have Vision?

Unlike the Mission Statement that clearly describes what you do and who you serve, a Vision Statement creates a desired outcome of future growth and deepening of service that is meant to inspire and energize your staff and board. A comprehensive and clearly defined Vision Statement sets the parameters of how the organization sees itself in the future and clearly describes how the organization will look so it knows when the vision is achieved.

2

Mission and Vision - Our Reason for Being

Every organization that wishes to be competitive with other organizations with similar focus or service populations needs to have a vision of what the future of their organization looks like. More importantly, this must be a shared vision with ownership by both the professional staff and members of the board of directors. In order to challenge the organization, this vision should be audacious and seek to elevate the agency, its board, and staff to the highest level of consciousness in moving toward the future. Once again, the emphasis in the organization's vision should be on moving toward becoming totally proactive in its approach to growth and development of the organization. Being able to fully understand the difference between a proactive and a reactive organization is a must in fashioning the Vision Statement. The following tables clearly show the difference between a reactive and a proactive organization. Using the creation of a Vision Statement to drive your planning creates the foundation upon which all decisions are made. Proactive organizations will succeed and reactive organization will most certainly fail.

Proactive Organization	Reactive Organization
Embraces change	Resists change
Aggressively seeks opportunities	Strives to maintain a level of comfort
Sees change as an opportunity for growth	Sees change as an obstacle to success
Is moved to action	Is frozen in fear
Uses outcomes to drive the resource development plan	Allows available resources to limit outcomes
Assesses, plans, and secures resources	Struggles to secure resources to maintain current level of service
Focuses on what needs to be done	Focuses is on fixing what has already happened
Challenges its board and staff to excel	Accepts mediocrity through complacency
Strives to meet the emerging needs of a changing community	Settles for current programs disregarding new community needs
Controls its own destiny	Survives at the mercy of its funders
Takes action which creates a feeling of freedom and puts the organization in control	Allows the organization to be immobilized by fear that paralyzes the mind, body, and spirit

As you can plainly see, the reactive organization is one embroiled in constant turmoil and consumed with daily survival. It is virtually impossible to formulate and execute a Vision Statement if you are constantly focused on putting out fires and just getting from week to week. The Strategy Development process takes a reactive organization and empowers it with the knowledge and commitment of staff and board to move toward a shared vision of the future. It identifies the key strategies that can and must be addressed within a reasonable period of time. It develops the goals and objectives to stimulate the organization to achievement rather than languish in mediocrity. It clearly assigns the responsibility to interdisciplinary teams made up of board and staff who are charged with the execution of the plan and more importantly are held accountable for their actions or inactions. Finally, it sets the table with additional strategic issues that have been prioritized so that once one strategy is completed successfully, another is waiting in the wings, which means the organization is constantly moving forward and not looking back.

It has been said, "Real perfection is in the striving to be perfect that leads you to set new goals and objectives which just keeps it out of reach." The Strategy Development process is built on this exact premise. Once your organization has achieved the initial goals it has set to help drive it toward the vision for the future, another is already waiting to be addressed. This is a dynamic process built on forward motion and never allows an organization to become satisfied and static. This constant forward motion toward the vision creates synergy and excitement among the staff and board and becomes a key motivator in attracting new board members and investors who want to be part of the dynamic process that defines your nonprofit.

Vision Is About More Than Growth

You should not imply from this chapter that to have a vision for the future always means significant growth. While growth is often seen as progress, nonprofits can run into problems understanding the long-term effects of such a strategy. Keeping this in mind, I think that the ideal concept of *vision* needs to have a clearly defined element of controlled growth but should also include a very specific element relating to the improvement in the quality of services your agency provides and how you measure that improvement in quality. One of the most exciting aspects of a consultant's job is when you are conducting a retreat

2

relative to Strategy Development and the discussion turns to both growth and quality. One can almost see the lights go on in the minds of some staff and board members as they come to the realization that growth and improvement in the quality of the services provided are not mutually exclusive but go hand in hand.

When mapping the Strategy Development process the agency follows a carefully prescribed sequence of activities that leads the organization from the preliminary discussion of mission through the final decisions on which strategic issues will be addressed first. Likewise, when establishing the goals and objectives for these strategic issues, prioritization and sequence become the catch words that ensure that form follows function. In the final analysis, the plan that is created and the vision for the future that is derived from it is not even worth the paper on which it is written if the mechanisms and buy-in from the staff and board are not present so there is no defined set of goals, objectives, or method for evaluation.

A Final Thought

Much has been discussed in this chapter relative to the Strategy Development process, the establishment of a comprehensive Mission Statement, and the creation of a Vision Statement. These are all very important components in moving your organization to action and keeping it focused on continual and steady forward progress. However, a chapter on Mission and Vision would be incomplete without discussing the quality and dedication of the professional staff of the organization and that of the board of directors. There is ample discussion throughout the remainder of this book that delves into the issues of developing quality staff and recruiting the right people to be on the board of directors. The point needed to be made here is that a deep-seated, emotional and passionate belief in what you do is absolutely necessary to the successful attainment of your mission and to move your organization in a positive way to achieve its vision.

It has been my great pleasure to work with some of what I consider the best and most dedicated staff and board members in a variety of organizations. The one common thread that binds them together is a deep-seated belief in what their organization does and how they do it. The emotional commitment that they make to the organization, although it is not paraded as a badge of honor, drives them to make their nonprofit succeed. Their passionate support each and every day serves as a shining light that attracts others to invest their time, energy, and financial resources as well. An organization can have an incredibly strong Strategic Initiative, it can have excellent services, and it can even have public acclaim for the work that it does; nevertheless, without this inner circle of core believers, it cannot and will not be able to attract new leaders and investors who will ultimately be needed to achieve its vision and execute its mission to the highest level.

Mission and vision are two very different components that are both necessary to your success as a nonprofit organization. It is incumbent upon your organization to define them, develop a plan for their achievement, and most importantly create the synergy necessary to ensure that they drive your organization in a consistent and dynamic fashion toward its destiny and to ensure you maximize the impact and outcomes of your nonprofit and those you are charged with serving.

Further information, tools, and services are available at www.theperfectnonprofit.com

2

*Mission and Vision -
Our Reason for Being*

Professional Leadership - the Art of Leading from Behind

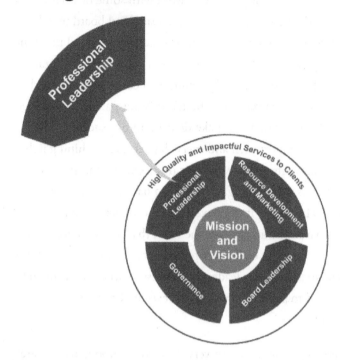

The art of being a successful nonprofit executive has been tried by many and mastered by few. Serving as the lead professional for a nonprofit organization requires one to focus on many different facets of operation and administration at the same time. One of the key facets mentioned in this book is balance. Balance is vital to being a successful executive in the nonprofit sector. Bum Phillips, a coaching icon in Texas, once said of his profession, "There's two kinds of coaches out there, those that's fired and those that's going to be fired." Do not let his words scare you, but this analogy can be indicative of the life of an agency executive if they do not operate at a meaningful and effective level.

Throughout the years of working with nonprofit executives, I have had the opportunity to work with many who came from a for-profit industry. They came into these nonprofit management jobs feeling that they were going to work part-time toward retirement. Those of you seasoned agency executives know where the story goes. The executives coming from the for-profit world without fail will tell you that leading a nonprofit is as challenging as leading a for-profit organization. While the success rate of these folks is high, they learn early on that running a nonprofit is anything but a retirement job. The agency executive must perform core tasks that are vital to the success of the organization. As always, especially in the nonprofit circles, there are exceptions to these tasks, but these exceptions should be few and far between. It is my humble opinion if these core tasks are adhered to, the nonprofit executive will be successful in carrying out the mission and vision of the organization.

Core Tasks of the Agency Executive

Functions of Agency Executive

Effectively Manage the Day-to-Day Operations of Your Organization

3

Whether you administer an advocacy group or you manage a charity that opens its doors to clients daily, weekly or monthly, there are day-to-day activities of an organization that must be tended to. Any agency executive or board member with any formal training at all knows this is a function that must be carried to a successful end by the executive professional. This is unequivocally the responsibility of professional staff. Again, this is NOT the responsibility of the board.

Many nonprofit executives tend to focus on what they feel is important for the organization. This can be a slippery, slimy slope. The strategic direction of the organization must be set by the board of directors. This does not mean that you as the executive will not be involved in the process; rather, it simply means as the lead professional of the organization your job is to carry out the strategic path of the organization as directed by the board. I cite this first because many agency executives fail to see this as a key part of the success of the organization. If executives drive the strategic thrust of the organization without board input, the organization will not see long-term success. Long-term success is defined differently than most would like. As explained in the board development chapter, if you are an executive running the inverted model of leadership, eventually the organization will struggle. This may come as a result of retiring, leaving for another opportunity, or being asked to leave by the board.

As I previously stated, managing the day-to-day operations of a nonprofit organization is very important. This is particularly of importance if you have a staff of people who are charged with carrying out the mission of the organization. If this is the case, it is vital that you clearly know and understand human resources and the effects of staffing in the workplace. Whether you manage a staff of two or two hundred, human resource management becomes a very integral role in your job. If your organization is at this level, it is strongly recommended that you have written policies and procedures to address almost any human resource issue. While people are vital to ensuring the success of a nonprofit organization, people can also cause problems within the organization. The effective agency executive will always be on top of human resources and the day-to-day operations of the organization.

3

Create Synergy with the Board

This is probably the most important part of the slippery, slimy slope I mentioned earlier. I can tell you with much surety that if you as an executive do not work closely with and develop positive relationships with your board, you will not succeed in your organization. More importantly, if you do hang on for many years as the Napoleonic figure of the organization, when you leave it will struggle mightily. This may seem somewhat averse to some of you. I would venture to guess in my twenty-three years of nonprofit management that 70 percent of the agency executives who lost their jobs did so because they failed to build relationships with their volunteer board people. Please understand that whether you are in an inverted, micromanagement or a balanced model of governance, it is unequivocal that the board of directors is the final authority on happenings of your organization. It is of little or no consequence whether the board is capable of handling this or not. It is a fact they are and always will be the final authority within an organization.

While many executives see boards as a necessary evil, I beg to differ. It seems in many cases, the agency executive feels the need to be in constant opposition to the board. This does not have to be the case. If your leadership qualities will allow you to share the mission and vision of the organization with the board, you and the board can be extremely successful. In reality, for the long-term viability of the organization, you must engage with

18

the board at a high level and if necessary, build the board to the level that it can govern your organization.

Many executives fall into the trap of believing when an individual steps on the board to serve, they know their roles and responsibilities. Serving on the board is no different than starting a new job. There needs to be an orientation and a learning curve. Once this has been achieved, board members can truly step up and govern the organization. Many times while boards are evolving, this is the job of the executive. Its members, good and bad, need the time to develop and become good board members. Again, as the agency executive, depending on the evolution of your board, this may be your responsibility. If you remain patient as the executive and aid the board in its evolution, you will be highly successful.

At the end of the day, managing board relations means picking up the pieces when they need to be picked up and moving forward.

Assure Financial Transparency and Viability

Money talks! Many of us in the nonprofit sector believe in the goodness of organizations and communities. Our hope would be that money would never introduce itself into the equation of operating a nonprofit. Reality tells us though that money and a nonprofit's effectiveness in managing and handling of finances is very important. In this instance, I must cite something that is very important in today's world. It will remain important for many years to come. Trust and public trust are really all that matters where finances are considered in a nonprofit. Many times, nonprofits get blamed for mismanagement or lack of transparency when they really have done nothing wrong. It is also vital to have proper policies and procedures in place to ensure the organization is managed and governed correctly from a financial perspective.

Assuring the financial wherewithal of the nonprofit organization seems to be difficult for many nonprofit agency executives. This occurs because many of those chosen as executives come from the nonprofit background from which there is no real learning center designed to teach people to manage finances. As the agency executive, particularly in a smaller nonprofit, I urge you to not get yourself stuck in a bad financial situation. It is easy to engage certified public accountants and other qualified bookkeepers to help manage the financial affairs of the organization. In the final analysis, it is the charge of the board to assure the finances are accurately explained and documented. Many nonprofit executives do not have strong financial backgrounds. If you do not have a background in this area, make sure you get the proper assistance from financial professionals. This is not an area in which you can afford any missteps.

Implement Organizational Goals and Objectives

Developing and implementing goals or objectives that drive the organization are vital in measuring the success of not only the organization but the effectiveness of the agency executive. Every nonprofit organization should have in place goals and objectives designed to drive the organization to the successful implementation of its mission and vision. Many times as agency executives, we get caught up in the minutia of carrying out the day-to-day operations of the organization. If the day-to-day operations of the organization are not tied in and closely aligned with a tactical or strategic plan, the efforts of the organization may be lost. The strategic or tactical direction of the organization should be planned by the board in conjunction with the agency executive and professional staff. Without a doubt, the job of implementing the tactical or strategic plan of the organization falls to the professional staff led by the agency executive.

Assuring the plan is in place to drive organizational objectives is essential not only to the success of the agency but to also show the worthiness and the effectiveness of the executive and professional staff of the organization. Again, depending on the status of your organization, you may need a tactical or strategic plan. Without question, the fact remains you must put one of these plans in place.

Assure Effective Governance

The Perfect Nonprofit Model as explained in this book details the four key components that surround mission and vision. It is obvious the agency executive plays a role in all of the key components. The way in which a nonprofit organization conducts its business and governs itself is vital to the success of the organization. It goes without saying that if an organization cannot conduct an effective board meeting within the confines of the bylaws of the organization, the organization will not be effective.

Again, someone has to assure that the organization operates in a fashion that is aimed at building trust with professional staff, members of the board, and the community. If the board is operating at a satisfactory level, it will assure that the governance model of the organization is followed. If this is not the case, the agency executive must perform this function. It matter not how much good is performed on a daily basis if the covenants of the organization are not followed.

The nonprofit that develops a sound governance structure to drive the organization will be leaps and bounds ahead of others. For some reason, in the nonprofit sector, many organizations do not form a solid governance structure. This is yet another shortfall that besets nonprofits when they go to the community for support. As simple a task as setting the governance model in place may be, organizations tend to not execute when it comes to governance. Many nonprofits start very small with a tight group of people implementing the mission and vision of the organization. These groups tend to see no need to develop any type of governance structure because of the ease of making decisions. In reality, this is the best and easiest time to set the governance structure in place and let it be a catalyst to lead the organization while it grows. In addition, if the organization is new, the leadership should be very familiar with the governance model. This is included in the articles of incorporation and by-laws that most nonprofits must file to receive their nonprofit status from the United States Treasury Department. If you ask, "What is our governance model?" very simply go to your organization's constitution and by-laws. It all resides there. In the end, you must drive this if the board is not at a place to do so.

Know Your Customer

Who is your customer? Is it your client who is receiving direct support from your organization? Is it the donors who financially support the agency? Is your customer the board of directors that employs you? It is your staff? Is your customer the volunteers in the community who assure that the organization meets its mission and vision? I could go on for quite awhile. The reality is that anyone your organization touches in any way is your customer. I am sure you have heard the old saying, "The customer is always right." This is as important to the nonprofit sector as it is to the for-profit sector.

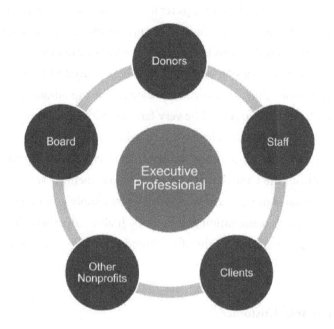

Customers

Again, I may be speaking out of place, but I believe each nonprofit organization has what I call key stakeholders in which the agency executive must invest time and effort. I have taken the liberty to list these below:

Donors

This is obvious, but it can be a blind spot for executives. Donors to your organization are like anyone else. If you do not pay attention to and cultivate them, they will go away. If people quit giving to your organization, it is sometimes difficult to get them back as a donor. After all, they stopped giving to your organization. Typically, donors will quit giving for a few reasons. First, they may want to focus their finances on some other type of project. Second, they may stop giving because you just simply did not ask. Lastly, they may not give because they have become disenchanted with the organization. None of the examples cited above are acceptable. Stewardship and ongoing cultivation of donors is very important to any organization, unless you just do not need money to operate your organization.

Professional Staff Members

If you operate a nonprofit and you employ professional staff, they too are your customer. Many executives will disagree and say that staff people are employees; therefore, they are paid to do the job for which they have been hired. However, my first question would be, "Do you want to have staff members who are enthusiastic and enjoy their job?" My hope would be that your answer would be, "Yes." This makes for a better work environment for all involved. Professional staff members can also cause you and your organization time and trust if they are not handled in a professional manner. Lastly, if you are the professional executive of the organization, your staff wants to hear from you! They want to know what your thoughts and strategies are for the organization. I understand that many of you may be running organizations with many employees. Please understand one thing. There is only one executive leader of the organization. People, especially your staff, want to hear from you! They are, in fact, your customer.

Board Members

This has already been touched on, but it cannot be mentioned enough. You must understand, the board of directors, in most cases, is the custodian of the organization. Therefore, they hold your collective fate in their hands. Period. End of discussion. Board members are your customer, and they always will be your customer. Working closely and building relationships with them can be some of the most rewarding work you can do. A final thought on the board being a customer is that it is okay to share the vision and mission of the organization with these people. They can make you look real good, and you can make them look like saviors to the community, if you will just commit to work with them.

Clients

All nonprofits are providing a product or service to those who
are in need of that particular product or service. I hope this is
implied, while I understand that there are exceptions to the
rule. Those with who you are charged with serving are always
your customer. These folks must always be treated with respect
and dignity no matter what the circumstance. Please, whatever
you do, never look down your nose at those you are charged
with serving. If people do not partake of the services your
organization is offering, this could present a large problem.

Other Nonprofit Organizations

This is the age of collaboration. Everyone is talking about
partnering. As the executive professional, you must be involved
with other agencies within your service area. This can also give
you and your organization exposure that is probably much
needed. I know there are those independent operators out there
who have all of the answers to all of the questions facing the
nonprofit sector. If you are one of these people, get involved in
your community! Share these strategies and ideas. Believe me,
you will get all of the credit for helping other organizations
build their capacity to serve the community. In the final
analysis, this equals better services, which then makes better
communities. Is that not the meaning of nonprofits?

The Perfect Nonprofit Executive

We have covered the tasks the executive must address to be
successful above. The last topic I would like to cover in this very
important chapter is simple. What are the attributes that make
a top-notch nonprofit executive? Let us look at our best view of
these attributes.

Exhibit Humility

It matters not who you are or what you tell others you are because no one likes a "know-it-all." When you present yourself as a humble person who speaks only when you have something positive to say, you will be on your way to gaining the respect of all of those you work with, except the "know-it-alls."

Create Organizational Synergy

Synergy is defined by some as the whole being greater than the sum of its parts. I could not describe it any more eloquently. As *The Perfect Nonprofit* executive, you must create this synergy within your organization. Once you create synergy with your customers, your organization will go to greater heights and will not suffer as many organizations do with the little things.

Focus on the Important

Success equals focusing on what is important. If you as the executive leader of the organization can maintain that focus and get your board and other professional staff members to focus on what is important, you will always have a productive and mostly rewarding workplace experience.

Ensure Balance

Obviously you have seen this word many times in the book because we are predicating the model on balance. It makes sense; *The Perfect Nonprofit* executive will exhibit balance at the workplace. In addition, the agency executive must exercise balance between work and personal time. Please read this carefully. **If you do not have a personal life that is fulfilling, you will not be as successful and productive at administering your nonprofit.** Every agency executive will work endless hours, and the work to be done by the organization is endless. It was best summed up to me in this way many years ago: "It will be

3

here when you get back. Go home and be with your family." This was told to me when I was at the apex of burnout in running a nonprofit organization. My boss, the board president, ordered me to do this. Yes, I was there, and it is not a pleasant place. If you do nothing but work, you will become resentful and you will burn out. Balance is the key.

Find Value in Everyone

Your job is to find value in everyone who is involved in your organization. Once you identify that value, you need to communicate it to the person. I am not saying you should go to a person on your staff and make them feel they will be the next savior to the organization, but kind words go a long way in making people feel confident and enabled. This creates great value in the organization because these people you value will be tireless in their efforts to promote the organization.

As is the case with many of the aspects mentioned throughout this book, this seems simple, but very few people seem to make it a practice. Being inclusive and making those involved in your organization feel good about what they are doing creates a great environment to address the mission and vision of the organization.

If the agency executive combines the attributes mentioned above while assuring they take care of the main functions of the organization, the nonprofit organization can reach great heights.

Further information, tools, and services are available at www.theperfectnonprofit.com

Resource Development and Marketing - Where the Rubber Meets the Road

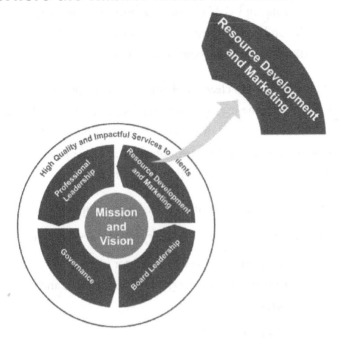

Resource Development and Marketing - Where the Rubber Meets the Road

Resource Development

Resource Development is on the lips of every nonprofit professional and volunteer from the time they get involved with a nonprofit organization. Yet in researching the web to come up with a simple definition of *resource development*, no clear example could be found. This, in and of itself, is not surprising. In fact, it underscores one of the primary problems most nonprofit agencies have in developing a comprehensive plan to address a concept that is clearly misunderstood. If you were to ask most nonprofit agencies for their definition of resource development, undoubtedly the very first thing they would mention would be money. For the vast majority of nonprofits, raising money is the one and only concept they associate with the term *resource development*. This is not only a disservice to the agency and those who they serve but it creates problems for the volunteer leadership of the organization by assigning them a singular focus that does not address the greater good of the agency.

28

The concept of resource development is so much more than just raising money. Having said this, it is absolutely true that for you to have a strong and viable agency you must raise money. How you do this and how you integrate this process into the overall organizational plan is the focus of this chapter.

Assuming there is no clear-cut definition for the process of resource development as a whole, let's take a moment to define the various components that make up a successful resource development program. Our own broad-based definition of resource development includes the following:

- Human resources and leadership development

- Mission-driven planning for resource development

- It's all about the investors: investor identification, cultivation, recruitment, acknowledgement, and retention

- Community collaboration

Resource Development Model

It is easy to see that while the majority of these components have raising money as their primary focus, there are others that speak to the issue of the human resources, planning, research, marketing, knowledge, and collaboration that are absolutely necessary to ensuring your success. For purposes of clarification, let's take each one of these components, define them, and assign them to one of several categories that will help you develop a successful plan.

Human Resources and Leadership Development

The single-most important key in successful fundraising, whether you are running a spaghetti dinner, a black-tie gala, an annual campaign, or a multimillion dollar capital/endowment campaign is leadership.

The American Heritage Dictionary defines leadership as **"lead·er·ship** n.

1. Capacity Capacity or ability to lead: *showed strong leadership during her first term in office.*

2. Guidance; direction: *The business prospered under the leadership of the new president."*

The role of a leader in a nonprofit organization is based not only on their capacity and ability to provide leadership, but also to provide the direction the organization needs to be continually moving forward to better fulfill their mission. Leadership in terms of resource development comes from a variety of sectors. There is the leadership provided by the executive, the board president, and, more importantly, there is the vast pool of leadership from the community at large that often goes untapped when it comes to resource development and the average nonprofit agency. The successful nonprofit has a clear understanding of the roles and relationships between these three groups. The board chairperson must not only understand his or her role and the role of the board, but must ensure that this role is carried out. The board's fundamental role is to set policy

Resource Development and Marketing - Where the Rubber Meets the Road and to raise the necessary resources needed by the organization to succeed. The role of the executive professional is to assist the board in the fulfillment of their responsibilities and also to administer the organization relative to the policies set by the board and within the resource base provided that is articulated in the annual budget. The community leader's roles are to recognize what agencies are having the greatest impact and assisting the volunteer and professional leadership in providing the resource needed to ensure this impact.

Every component of resource development requires that someone step up and take responsibility for not only driving the success of the effort but also for delegating authority and responsibility for the tasks that will need to be accomplished if success is to be realized. The mark of a truly great leader is to have the insight and intelligence to define these tasks, but also the strength of character and the security within themselves to delegate the responsibility for each and the authority to carry them out. When it comes to providing the leadership for successful resource development, everyone must park their personalities and egos at the door. A wise man once said, "There is no 'I' in TEAM"! This is never truer than in the leadership dynamics of a nonprofit agency. The minute ego and personality are allowed to creep into the equation, the more likely the effort at hand will fail.

The most effective resource development initiatives are symbiotic relationships between the organization, the community, and the people who have stepped forward to lead the way. The process of symbiosis allows for each partner to derive a benefit from the partnership. In the case of nonprofits, each successful resource development initiative provides the ongoing support it needs to carry out its mission. The community derives the direct benefit of being the recipient of the programs and services prescribed in that mission, as well as the feeling of goodwill from investing in itself. The leadership derives the feeling of satisfaction in a job well done and knowing that they have made their community a better place to live. For your agency to strive for perfection, it is critical to have each contributor clearly understand the investment they are making in their community and how this investment is improving the quality of life, not only for the population they serve, but for the entire community as well. Too often the focus of every resource development effort becomes the raising of the money itself and not the outcomes that will be derived by competent stewardship of those funds.

Resource Development and Marketing - Where the Rubber Meets the Road

Dynamic leadership not only provides this focus but also provides the necessary tools to bring this message to the community-at-large and the resolve to ensure its success. Some of the characteristics of great leadership include the ability to communicate the message; the ability to inspire those around them; the talent to break down a complex project into its most elemental parts; and the ability and willingness to identify and recruit those people who are best suited to address each of these elementary components.

In twenty-four years working as a resource development consultant, I can say unequivocally that the degree of success or failure of every project I have worked on lies directly with the caliber and abilities of the individuals who stepped forward to lead the effort. As stated earlier, there are many variables when launching any resource development effort. Your organization can agonize over each and every one and come up with compromises for most of them that will work. However, there is one and only one where there can be no compromise: LEADERSHIP! If you want your spaghetti dinner, your raffle, your black-tie gala, your annual campaign, and even your multi-million dollar capital campaign to succeed, there is one and only one way to ensure that success — The Right Leadership.

The Perfect Example: Leadership Inspires and Produces

One of my favorite anecdotes relative to leadership is a man who was identified as the best potential leader to chair an organization's capital campaign in the Feasibility Study. However, this man had no affiliation or relationship with the organization in question. After much research and talking with people from all walks of the community who knew this man, an appointment was set to try and recruit him. By virtue of the position he held with his company and the success it has achieved, it was clear this was the man we wanted to chair the drive. The recruitment was done at the organization. While visiting with the kids, this man came alive and clearly saw the benefit to the community for such an agency. After accepting the role of General Chairman, he spent a considerable amount of time learning about the organization and what they did for kids. His leadership skills along with his selfless attitude of getting the job done created a leadership team made up of people outside the board of directors that was second to none. He ended every meeting with a simple phrase: "Failure is not an option." Not only did this become the rallying motto for the campaign, but it became imbedded in every member of the team. This gentleman who went from no knowledge of the organization to General Chairman to devoted volunteer not only ensured the project's success but brought it in millions of dollars over goal.

Mission-Driven Planning for Resource Development

Regardless of the revenue-generating event or process you

choose, if the achievement of your mission is not the central focus, it will fail. People must clearly understand how, why, and what their investment in the organization will be used for and what impact it will ultimately have on them and the community in which they live. You must be able to articulate the Return on Investment (ROI) in order to get people to invest in the first place. There is an old adage, "You define your mission and your mission defines you." This is critical if you are to strive toward becoming *The Perfect Nonprofit*.

Your mission is not just words on a piece of paper or a plaque that hangs on the wall. Your mission must be the living, breathing manifestation of what you do each and every day in your organization. This mission should be internalized in every staff person, every board member, and must be the single focus that drives all of your resource development efforts. In today's modern world, with the stresses and pressures that are of each and every citizen, the decision to part with their hard-earned cash to help your organization by necessity must strike a chord in their heart. It is your mission that defines who and what you are. It must communicate clearly the focus of your efforts and the impact those efforts will achieve.

There is a new and exciting category of nonprofit investors today called *Social Entrepreneurs*. These are successful men and women who look upon supporting nonprofit organizations as an investment and they need to know going in what the return on their investment will be. You need only read the newspaper to understand the focus of this new class of nonprofit supporter. There are stories appearing daily relative to social entrepreneurs like Bill Gates, Warren Buffet, Ted Turner, etc. While you may not have investors of this magnitude in your community, I can assure you that these social entrepreneurs do exist in your communities and they will make substantial investments in you as long as you can articulate the return on investment.

It's All About the Investors: Investor Identification, Cultivation, Recruitment, Acknowledgement, and Retention

4

It must be clearly understood that resource development cannot occur if there are no resources. Resources in this case do refer to the money you need to achieve your goals. "We know we need it, we know where it is, but how do we get people to give it to us?" The very first thing you need to do is stop using the word give. Your organization is a business with a specific product, defined by a mission with measurable outcomes, and provides a return on investment for all of those who invest. Instilling the concept of investment/return on investment in your organization is the first major step in launching a culture change within your organization that will lead it to success. While this may seem to be a semantic issue, I can assure you it is not. Once the organization has made this cultural shift, the ability for it to attract investors will improve and help it achieve its goals.

There are five key components to finding, attracting, convincing, and maintaining investors.

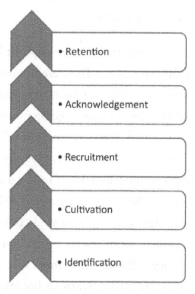

- Retention
- Acknowledgement
- Recruitment
- Cultivation
- Identification

Investor Relationship Model

First you need to identify who your potential investors are. This is best done through a prescribed process called investor identification and rating. This process can and should be made up of multidisciplinary teams of board members and community-at-large volunteers whose sole purpose is to identify potential investors and determine their capacity to invest. Individual, corporate, and foundation research can be done by staff to provide the information needed to be used in this process, but the key to success is in the individualized knowledge of those who serve on this committee. One of the primary advantages to identifying and rating investors in this way leads to the second key component of success: attracting the investor.

As each potential investor is identified and rated, the team should also identify the single-best person who can help recruit the prospect to invest. This is the first step in cultivating that prospect to, in fact, invest in your organization. In order to recruit this prospect as an investor, they need to know about your organization, what is does, and how it will not only benefit the community but what the return on investment is for them. Getting the investor this firsthand knowledge often relies on getting the recruiter identified by the investor ID committee to provide them with some basic information but more importantly to get them to visit your organization and get the knowledge directly.

This visit then is the first step in the formal recruitment process and should involve a recruitment team made up of the recruiter, the board chairperson, the executive professional and, if possible, someone from your agency who has benefited from your programs and services who can personalize the outcomes you are achieving. This team should be knowledgeable, focused, motivated, and know specifically who will make the request of the prospect to invest and when this occurs. The recruitment team should also have a leader who orchestrates the visit and has developed key signals for the remainder of the team as to

4

the timing of the ask or if more cultivation is needed. Assuming you get the investor to commit to invest in your agency, the scope and magnitude of the investment needs to be defined with the investor's level of investment recorded on an Intent to Invest Form signed by the investor.

The acknowledgement of this investment is the first practical and necessary step in maintaining the interest of the investor and perhaps increasing the level of investment from year to year. In order to achieve and maintain investor confidence, you must keep the investor informed at all times of the outcomes you are deriving from his or her investment, what the return on the investment is and how it has been determined.

The importance of frequent informational updates without asking for another investment is critical to the process of maintaining the investor's commitment and focus. Once they have achieved an initial investment, too many organizations seek to escalate it prematurely or fail to maintain contact with the investor and then wonder why the investment is not renewed.

Show Me the Money

The process of raising money for your organization can be divided into two key components: "How are you going to raise it?" and "What you are going to raise money for?" As every nonprofit is aware, there are a limited number of focal points for fund raising efforts. These include operations, capital, endowment, programs/services, debt reduction, and special projects. Literally all aspects of the funds needed to maintain and operate a successful nonprofit can be included in one of these primary areas. The amount of money that can be raised for each of the key components is dependent upon the need that can be established, the leadership that can be recruited to execute it, the primary resource pool of investors, the immediacy of the cause, the reputation of the agency, and the return on investment that can be established for each.

Special Events and Sales

As to how agencies choose to raise their money, there appears to be a simple pattern that has developed over the years. The majority of nonprofit agencies tend to gravitate toward events and sales as primary tools for raising funds. This is due in part because people feel comfortable in selling a ticket to an event, a raffle ticket, or some form of product rather than just asking people for money. However, a curious dichotomy occurs with this thinking. To raise money using an event and/or sale as the primary vehicle immediately builds in a substantial expense side to the equation. Therefore, in order to raise the original amount the agency needed, they actually have to raise substantially more money in order to cover the expenses for raising the money. This can create problems and in some cases becomes a self-fulfilling prophecy of failure. While you may incur minor costs in making a face-to-face ask (materials, transportation, consulting costs, etc.), these will be minor in relation to the amount of money you can raise. There is little doubt that the single-best means to raise substantial dollars for your organization is by making an intelligently prospected, research-founded personal approach to making the ask with the best person possible seeking the investment from the prospect for your agency. What vehicle you choose to raise the money you need oftentimes will dictate the ultimate amount you will raise. An entire book can be written on how to plan, execute, and define every fund raising event or vehicle used by nonprofits throughout the years. In fact, there are books on every aspect of how to raise money. *The Perfect Nonprofit* is currently developing manuals as a supplement to this book that will cover each avenue of fund raising in detail, providing you with the specific goals, objectives, policies, and procedures that will carry you to success.

If determining how you are going to raise money impacts how

4

Resource Development and Marketing - Where the Rubber Meets the Road

much you raise then certainly what you are raising it for will have an even greater impact on the total you attain. In terms of the ease of raising money for your agency, I don't think you will find many people who think any kind of fundraising is easy. However, there are certain objectives that, while not easy, can be facilitated better than others. Perhaps the single-most difficult, if not impossible, focus to raise money for is debt reduction. This is more than likely due to the perception that if you have had to incur debt to operate or provide facilities, you probably have not done a very good job in raising funds or managing the funds you have raised. This may not be true but a primary principle in all fundraising is that "Perception is reality."

Endowment

Raising dollars through a campaign strictly for endowment is very difficult. Many people, including the social entrepreneurs who were mentioned earlier, do not feel comfortable in giving you their money to manage and invest so you can generate operating dollars. For the most part, these donors would rather invest the money themselves and provide you the funds for a specific purpose by investing in your organization. Most successful endowment campaigns are based on constituent giving from people who either benefited from, or are benefiting from, the programs and services you provide. College alumni who currently may have children attending the same university are prime examples of this type of giving. It has been our experience that if you can tie in an endowment campaign to a carefully structured and executed capital campaign, the chances for success increase dramatically.

Planned Giving

No one likes to confront their own mortality so discussing a planned gift with someone can be both tenuous and uncomfortable. This is one area where one of the participants seeking the investment of the planned gift should be familiar with all of the vehicles for planned giving and be able to explain their benefit to the prospect. In most cases, this will have to be a volunteer with a background in planned giving or a paid professional who both understands and can communicate what these various tools will do to help the prospect in their estate planning. This is a case where a little knowledge can be a dangerous thing. Unless you are a certified estate planner, an accountant, or a planned giving professional, no one working for or serving on the board of a nonprofit agency should ever render legal, financial, or planned giving advice to a prospect. Your own role in this process is to facilitate setting up the meeting and the players who can make a planned gift a reality. There are so many facets to making a planned gift that it is virtually impossible for anyone to understand them unless they are a planned giving professional. What is important is that planned gifts, like all appeals for support, need to start at home. Each member of the board of directors should carefully evaluate their own estate planning to determine where support of the organization fits in their personal planned gift or at the very least as part of their last will and testament. For purposes of planning, if the person's last will and testament is the vehicle chosen, the organization cannot and should not anticipate the gift in future budgeting or planning unless it is in the form of an irrevocable codicil to the will.

Resource Development and Marketing - Where the Rubber Meets the Road

Annual Campaign

Raising money for operations, specific programs and/or services, and for special projects usually falls within the parameters of those special events and sales approaches discussed earlier. However, as successful or unsuccessful these may be, the single-best way to ensure yearly annual revenue is through a comprehensively planned and executed annual campaign. The annual campaign process is much more than an annual appeal through the mail or your board members asking their friends for support. The annual campaign process when approached through a systematic, well-planned campaign can be the foundation for generating support for your annual operating costs each year and can build on itself until it becomes the single-most effective way to generate the revenue you need to operate.

Like any other campaign, an annual campaign should involve first and foremost support from your own board of directors. Next, if the campaign is to attain the monetary levels you need, you should seek leadership outside the board to serve as the governing body of the campaign. This external leadership can bring new and vibrant people to your table whose sole focus is the successful completion of the campaign. Prospecting, as discussed earlier, is even more important in a carefully structured annual campaign. Many people make the mistake of seeking only individuals to invest in their annual campaigns. However, the corporate/business community and local and regional foundations can and do play a significant role in the well-planned annual campaign.

Your annual campaign should have a built-in system of checks and balances, as well as a means of determining the status of every aspect of the process as it moves forward. Because your annual campaign will, by necessity, have to be completed in a finite period of time, each and every volunteer must know their role and execute it perfectly within the timeline allotted to them. For this reason alone, there needs to be constant oversight and communication with the volunteers working on the campaign. The goal you set for your annual campaign must be easily justified and articulated; furthermore, you should determine it is attainable once you have completed the prospecting for the drive. If there are not a sufficient number of gifts to attain your goal then you must modify the goal. The last thing your agency needs is to launch a campaign that is doomed to failure because of the lack of sufficient prospects. Once completed, the campaign volunteers and agency staff need to debrief, analyze, and evaluate what worked, what didn't, and what can be done better and the planning for next year's campaign begins immediately. Using this system not only helps to ensure the success of the current drive but helps it build on itself year after year until it becomes the dominant fundraising project supporting the organization.

Capital Campaigns

Last but not least in terms of our discussion on Show Me the Money is the Capital Campaign. The capital campaign process is perhaps the most misunderstood of all the various aspects of raising money. The term itself is the perfect descriptor, CAPITAL Campaign. The term capital refers to funds needed for capital improvements to facilities, equipment, property, vehicles, and any number of other goods or construction efforts that your nonprofit may need to provide the program and services you offer. Many organizations function under the erroneous thinking that a capital campaign will solve their operational funding issues. In fact, this could not be further from the truth. In order for an organization to consider launching a successful capital campaign, they must — and I emphasize the word MUST — have a stable operating budget. Your organization will need to demonstrate your capability as competent money managers in order to get people to provide you with the necessary level of giving to conduct a successful capital campaign. Ask yourself why anyone would want to give money to build new or renovated facilities when you cannot operate what you have now? The decision to conduct a capital campaign will undoubtedly be the most important yet frightening decision any nonprofit board will ever make. Yet this decision will also be the most fulfilling achievement of that same board when it succeeds. All things considered, a successful capital campaign will impact three to four generations of families that your organization serves.

It Takes a Village: Community Collaboration

4

Resource Development and Marketing - Where the Rubber Meets the Road

The days of the individual nonprofit empire are quickly fading into the past. The new catchphrases today when it comes to nonprofits are collaboration, partnership, and sharing. There is little doubt that the competition for investors is increasing at a dramatic rate while at the same time the number of investors may, in fact, be dwindling. Those nonprofits that wish to thrive and strive toward perfection are recognizing that they may not be able to do this alone. The entire process of collaboration speaks to the issue of cost effectiveness, continued solvency, and a desire to meet the needs of the community using a different model than has existed in the past. Investors and foundations are both looking at interagency cooperation and collaboration before they commit their funds. National foundations are now demanding that the applications for their support clearly demonstrate interagency collaboration and cooperation if they are to be funded. Perhaps the most interesting aspect of this new wave is the kinds of nonprofits that are partnering and collaborating. Organizations who in the past would not be caught dead even talking to a perceived competitor are now joining forces to address the emerging needs of their communities in collaborative harmony, which not only instills confidence in investing in them but also works to attract donors who may never have given to either organization. Nonprofit campuses are now springing up around the country where more than one agency can construct the specific facilities they need to implement their programs and services around a core building where services common to all partners can be shared. Nonprofit agencies are partnering with school districts to provide more comprehensive after-school care. Nonprofits are collaborating with other nonprofits to provide a boost to community service in a cost-effective and focused model of cooperation that inspires people and foundations to invest. Organizations serving very different constituencies are coming together in a symbiotic relationship that not only attracts their traditional investors but may actually entice new generations of investors through innovative and cutting-edge philosophies of service.

The Perfect Example: Special Olympics and a Boys & Girls Club

4

Two organizations had the need to increase and expand their services in a community. The community, most definitely had a need for a Boys & Girls Club for disadvantaged kids living there. Special Olympics had an exceptional outdoor recreation area with a world-class track but no indoor program space. The Boys & Girls Club was already in a very highly successful Capital/ Endowment Campaign. Special Olympics needed an infusion of youth into their organization, indoor programming space, and a new direction in their fundraising and the Boys & Girls Club needed land and a new focus within the community. The two agencies came together and collaborated on the building of a state-of-the-art, full-service Boys & Girls Club built on land owned by the Special Olympics. This collaboration not only created a synergistic organization providing the opportunity for cross training and programming, but also provided an opportunity to attract donors to a project that would not have inspired them to give if they had gone it alone. The end result was a state-of-the-art Boys & Girls Club on the Special Olympics campus, a highly successful campaign, but most importantly services being provided to kids from both the Boys & Girls Clubs and the Special Olympics at a level that could not have happened if they had tried to do this independently.

Resource Development: The Tangible vs. the Intangible for Your Organization

4

The following charts clearly delineate the tangible vs. intangible benefits of having a comprehensive resource development initiative for your organization. As most organizations only relate to resource development in terms of funds raised, this chart is very important to engage a board of directors in the multiplicity of reasons to undertake such an effort.

Tangible Resource Development Components	Intangible Resource Development Components
• Operational Funding	• Community Visibility
• Capital Funding	• Community Awareness
• Endowment Funding	• Community Understanding of the Organization's Mission
• Special Project Funding	
• Foundation Grants	• Board Development
• Corporate Funding	• Volunteer Recruitment
• Government Funding	• Donor Cultivation
• Special Events	• Donor Retention
• Annual Campaign	
• Collaborations	
• Partnerships	
• Sponsorships	
• Sustaining Memberships	

The Importance of the Internal Resource Development Audit

An Internal Resource Development Audit provides a baseline assessment of the strength of an organization's resource development programs and staff from which future planning can begin. The process of conducting an Internal Resource Development Audit parallels the developing of a Strategic Plan. Information is collected from a variety of sources in various formats from the organization's existing programs and materials. In addition, interviews are conducted with key personnel, board members, and non-board volunteers to assess their perception of the resource development program and to determine if they have a reality-based understanding of the needs of the organization. A Comprehensive Audit:

- Examines at the fiscal management of the organization, including operations (both income and expenses), resource development initiatives, and endowment

- Evaluates the accounting practices of the organization and compares them to standard accounting practices nationwide

- Assesses and analyzes the percentage of paid and volunteer human resources relegated to resource development

- Analyzes the actual return to the organization of current resource development effort

- Determines what further fund raising activity is required to meet their goals

The Resource Development Plan: I've Got a Plan, You've Got a Plan, Everybody Has to Have a Plan!

The information collected in the audit is then applied to a series of tests and can be included in the development of strategic issues that need to be addressed to move the agency forward. In doing this, the groundwork is laid for the creation of a Resource

Resource Development and Marketing - Where the Rubber Meets the Road

4

Development Plan that contains the guiding principles of the who, what, why, and when of the resource development program. This guidepost to resource development success is often overlooked, or worse ignored, by the average nonprofit organization and thus their resource development efforts lack focus, strength, and direction and ultimately wind up failing. The benefits of constructing such a plan include the following:

- Provides a road map to successful resource development

- Demonstrates to the community a professional response to addressing the needs of the organization

- Articulates the real needs of the organization

- Forces the organization to evaluate each aspect of its resource development program

- Provides the basis for achieving economic stability for the organization

- Ensures the future of the organization

A comprehensive resource development plan contains:

- The club's mission statement

- An analysis of the data collected during the internal resource development audit

- The goals for the plan based on the analysis (both short and long term)

- Specific measurable objectives (both short and long term)

- An action plan

- Appendices containing supporting data

The action plan includes:

- Specific methods to accomplish each objective

- Assignment of responsibilities for attainment of each objective

- The evaluation tools that will be used to measure attainment of the objectives

- A timeline that allows for a regularly scheduled review of the plan that then allows for modification and revision

- Appendices inclusive of all supporting data

Marketing as a Vital Tool in Resource Development

The Merriam Webster Dictionary gives the following definitions:

mar·ket·ing, *noun:* 1 a : the act or process of selling or purchasing in a market; b : the process or technique of promoting, selling, and distributing a product or service; 2 : an aggregate of functions involved in moving goods from producer to consumer.

public relations, *noun plural but usually singular in construction;* Usage: *often attributive;* **a:** the business of inducing the public to have understanding for and goodwill toward a person, firm, or institution; *b:* the degree of understanding and goodwill achieved.

It should be noted that public relations is but one component of effective marketing. Public Relations is a management function that evaluates public attitudes, identifies the politics of an individual or an organization within the public interest and then plans and executes a program of action geared at earning public understanding and acceptance. This means advising management on public reaction to possible management decisions, as well as the planning and dissemination of messages to the public(s), for the purpose of gaining support and understanding of the organization.

Peter Drucker said, "The aim of marketing is to know and understand the customer so well the product or service fits him and sells itself."

Marketing is the greatest enigma in the nonprofit world. Perhaps no other component of fund raising and getting your message to the community is more important yet routinely overlooked than marketing. There is one obvious and simple explanation for this. In the greater scheme of running a nonprofit organization, marketing is not an expense that is easily dealt with. In striving to keep the lights on, the staff paid, and the building heated, spending money on, marketing is the easiest area to cut. In working with nonprofit organizations for over twenty-four years, I can count on one hand the number of organizations who actually had a line item in their budget for marketing. Having established that marketing is not a priority for the majority of nonprofit agencies, let me make the case for why it should be. The old adage in business that "You have to spend money to make money" is even truer in the nonprofit world. Investors cannot and will not invest in your agency if they don't know about you. If they cannot understand or relate to the programs and services you provide and have a clear understanding of the outcomes their investment will generate, they will not invest. Most nonprofits serve their communities in relative obscurity because they relate marketing as an expensive proposition that utilizes paid advertising, electronic media, and costly ad campaigns. The reality is that nonprofit agencies can use a variety of nontraditional avenues to get their message out and not spend a lot of money.

Today we all live in the world of the internet, cell phones, computers, e-mail, television, radio, and any number of other media that impact the lives of every person, every day, in America. Perhaps no greater example of how this can be used in the raising of money can be found then in the campaign of our forty-fourth President, Barack Obama. President Obama, when just a candidate, used a process of social networking that not only got his message and agenda out to the masses but also was the focal point of a fund raising effort that raised the most money for one presidential candidate in history. This process is what enabled him to saturate the airways and media and that ultimately led to his election. While the magnitude of President Obama's approach is beyond the reach of local nonprofits, the concept is not. The primary ambassadors of your organization are its board of directors. Each member of the board has a rolodex, an e-mail contact list, or any number of other lists of friends and acquaintances that become the database from which to launch a modified version of the Obama model. Social networking is useful and potentially valuable in many ways, including:

- Connecting with clients and other stakeholders.
- Changing your communications to a more conversational mode instead of the one-way "publishing" approach of most communications to this point. .
- Shifting the culture of your organization to listen more... to clients and other stakeholders.
- Establishing a cost efficient way to build awareness.
- Friendraising... the first step in cultivation and relationship building.

Websites for your organization can not only carry your message but also serve as a means to keep your community updated on the outcomes it is achieving. Electronic newsletters can be published and sent to everyone in your community who provides an e-mail address and most certainly your entire donor base. Donated billboard space from local outdoor advertising companies can send a loud and clear message that you are here and doing your job. The creation of a speaker's bureau from within your board and staff can get your message to every service organization who has regularly scheduled meetings in your community. The cost of these to you is minimal.

4

Resource Development and Marketing - Where the Rubber Meets the Road

The Perfect Example: "Tom Sawyer Marketing" How to Get Somebody to Paint Your Fence

Cause-related marketing is a symbiotic relationship between two parties who each have something that can benefit the other and who have a means of entering into a partnership whereby both parties can achieve these benefits. The Story of Tom Sawyer is a perfect example. Tom was charged with painting his aunt's fence. He talked some of his friends into doing it by telling them how much fun he was having and how much fun it would be for him. They painted her fence while he lounged in the shade. Tom got what he wanted and his friends believed they were having fun. In today's modern nonprofit, we don't have to rely on deception to create cause-related marketing partnerships in order to secure what we need in marketing. The benefits to both parties can be both meaningful and dynamic, thus benefiting both partners. Some classic examples of this include the following:

- A car dealer who puts a simple declarative statement in his weekly advertising (e.g. "Proud Supporter of your organization." They become known for their charitable support and you get weekly exposure in the paper).

- A retailer who donates a portion of every sale to your charity during a specific promotion for a specified period of time and uses this in their advertising. This can draw people who support your agency into the business and you in turn share in the profits of this endeavor.

- A local merchant who sponsors a major event and uses her advertising to promote that event for your organization, dual exposure and the opportunity to attract people from your event into their business.

- A businessman who agrees to pay for your printing and promotional materials and gets to include his name and information as the donor on the back of the information piece. Recognized for their benevolence and fills one of your needs with a cost-effective contribution.

It should be clearly understood that marketing does not raise money, it raises consciousness! An effective marketing plan is a dynamic component of a comprehensive resource development plan. The critical element that ensures the success of both is consistency. There are clearly defined roles for both the staff and the board of directors. The tables below specifically outline these tasks.

Staff Responsibilities:

- Data collection
- Identification and validation of human interest stories
- Participation in marketing committee
- Point of contact for tours (face-to-face)
- Secures permission for member participation
- Provides support and focus

Board Responsibilities:

Resource Development and Marketing - Where the Rubber Meets the Road

- Participation in developing marketing plan

- Serve on marketing committee

- Creates and approves marketing budget

- Secures resources to execute plan

- Serve as ambassadors to the community

- Secures potential supporters for tours

- Provides the staff with resources necessary for success

The Perfect Example: "Party Marketing" Using the Board as Ambassadors

Many members of the board of directors attend meetings and events and are true believers in your cause. Each and every board member needs to be an ambassador for your organization every day. When attending a party and someone brings up a topic, it is not hard to relate that topic back to something you may be doing at your organization. For example, someone comments on the excellent quality of the food. The board member can talk about how good the quality of the food is that you are serving at the soup kitchen, the food bank, the dinner program for your organization, or the recipes being taught at the culinary arts program for single moms. Each and every interaction between your board members and the people in the community is an opportunity to talk about your nonprofit. This form of party marketing can be carried out at any number of venues and social functions with the cost to you zero; the impact to your organization great!

The Marketing process is cyclical in nature:

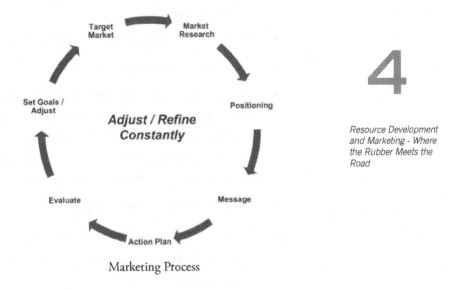

Marketing Process

Set Marketing Goals:

- Attainable
- Timed
- Targeted
- Evaluated
- Modifiable

Identify the Target Market: Decide who you are trying to reach:

- Clients
- Volunteers
- Donors – individual, corporate, foundation, government
- Employees/potential employees
- Community

Analyze the Market/Market Research: Know what your Target Market wants:

- The basic approach is the same for any target market

54

- Do not let your assumptions determine your marketing/message

- Ask your community (e.g. survey; focus group)

- Understand what is important to them

- Listen carefully to the people you are trying to reach (e.g., an organization markets to donors as serving poor, inner-city kids when donors want to hear that the organization serves all kids with particular emphasis on poor, inner-city kids)

- Focus on a few of the most important issues

- Know the competition and what they do

- Analyze SWOT (Strengths, Weaknesses, Opportunities, Threats)

Establish Positioning: Create a message about your value and uniqueness:

- Focus on things that are important to your community

- Keep the message simple

- Three to five key elements, not a laundry list

- Identify and communicate differentiators (why is your organization different from other similar agencies in town?)

- Be specific – numbers, outcomes, stories have power. Generic statements do not!

The Right Message: Your Mission:

- Who are you? What do you want to do?

- You define your mission and your mission defines you!

- Your mission should be clear and concise

- Total focus on what you are and what you want to do

- Your mission is NOT WORDS written on a page
- It is a living, breathing manifestation of the value you bring to your community
- It needs to be lived every day, NOT just reviewed once a year!

Action Plan: The necessary building blocks to a sound marketing program:

- Establish a plan of action
- Objectives
- Strategy
- Action Items
- Schedule
- Accountability
- Reporting/Measurement
- Evaluation
- Feedback Mechanism

Evaluate Impact: Never Make Assumptions:

- Establish a plan of action
- Objectives
- Strategy
- Action Items
- Schedule
- Accountability
- Reporting/Measurement
- Evaluation
- Feedback Mechanism

Adjust and Refine Constantly:

- Create a feedback loop

   o   Evaluate your marketing against goals

   o   Is it having the right impact?

   o   Survey target audience

   o   Adjust the marketing plan

- Don't rest on your laurels – your competition is not standing still

A future manual in *The Perfect Nonprofit* series will focus on developing a marketing plan. For now, suffice it to say that while marketing may not be a priority in your resource development plan now, there are ways to make it a cost-effective reality that will deepen the impact of your fund raising efforts.

The Final Test: Raising Money in Challenging Times

If nonprofits are to flourish in the coming century, they must identify the markets where they have the greatest chances for success. Individual philanthropy in this country is outdistancing corporate, business, government and foundation giving dramatically. While there is never a good time to raise money, the need for your services increases during challenging economic times and the availability of funding dwindles. You need to become even more aggressive in your fund raising efforts in down times. You have to be more aware of what your growing needs are and even more diligent in making sure you have a strong resource plan based on the following keys.

Keys to Raising Money in Times of Change

It is only through validation of your achievements that you demonstrate the return on investment to the social entrepreneurs who will fund you regardless of economic circumstances. Some nonprofit organizations actually retreat on fund raising during bad economic times when they should really be on the attack. While others withdraw from the fund raising arena, it is your opportunity to move your organization forward. While others worry, your resource development plan will position your organization to succeed.

You must use education as the great equalizer. Teach the community what you are doing and the impact you are having. Explain how your organization is serving even greater numbers in these troubled times and that you are truly making a difference in the lives of those you serve. Ask the donors for their understanding and back this up with the statistical analysis of your outcomes. Use cultivation as a tool that can and will make a difference as potential investors get used to hearing from your organization when you do not have your hand out. Help your community take ownership of the process of supporting your organization; let your board have ownership of the fundraising process and allow your staff to take ownership of providing the necessary information to make this approach work. Finally, always be on the lookout for recruitment of key partners from the philanthropic community, the business community, the foundation community, and the community of other nonprofits that can benefit from their association with you, and you with them.

4

Resource Development and Marketing - Where the Rubber Meets the Road

The Perfect Example: Henny-penny and the Sky is Falling

All of you will remember the childhood story of Henny-penny and her ability to convince her friends that the sky was falling. Henny-penny was so adamant in delivering this message that all her friends did in fact think that the sky was falling and life as they knew it would be destroyed. And they were right — life as they knew it soon was destroyed not by the fact that the sky fell but because in their zeal to spread the word they trusted Foxy-woxy who used the circumstances of their fear to victimize them and provide himself with a nice meal.

4

There are those in today's world who would have us believe that the sky is falling. The economy is in disarray, and it is easy for the media and others to create a picture of doom and gloom. And like Henny-penny and her friends, if that becomes the sole focus of our lives, life as we know it will be changed forever. However, it is my contention that if we allow this barrage of negativity to become the driving force in our lives, we will create a self-fulfilling prophecy of failure that will be near impossible to overcome. As nonprofit organizations, your workload, the need for your programs and services, and the positive impact you can have in the communities you serve will not cease to exist or be diminished because the economy is not all we want it to be. In fact, the reality is the need for what you do, how you do it, and the need for it only increases in a down economy when more people are forced to find help and services within the nonprofit world.

The need to focus on those who need you and the impact you can continue to have not only avoids a self-fulfilling prophecy of failure, it plants a seed of hope in the hearts of those you serve and those who support you and gives them a reason to feel positive. This is the antithesis of Henny-penny's message. You can make a conscious choice to embrace today's challenges and meet them head on or you can let fear of what might be paralyze both you, your volunteers, and those who might have supported you. You can focus on the increased need for your programs and services or you can prepare yourself to be Foxy-woxy's next meal. It's your choice; join the heard of those who fear tomorrow or grasp the opportunity that exists today to distinguish your organization from the rest and attack the problems of today knowing that tomorrow is just another day.

It is not impossible to raise funds in a down economy. It may take longer, you may have to seek more investors, and you may have to use additional planning and creativity but those organizations who make this investment of their time and energy will not only raise money now but will position themselves to be even more successful as the economy starts to rebound. These organizations that wait until that turn around starts will be left at the gate.

Further information, tools, and services are available at www.theperfectnonprofit.com

4

Resource Development and Marketing - Where the Rubber Meets the Road

Board Leadership - the Inexact Science

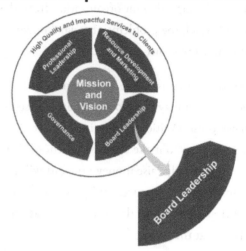

Boards and how they govern organizations are as diverse as the
most colorful rainbow. Although there are governance structures
available to anyone who really wants to investigate, which have
been proven to work, nonprofit organizations still tend to try
and recreate this wheel. In many cases, cultural views of boards
are defined within communities, but this is a dangerous way
to choose a governance model due to the diverse nature of
the nonprofit sector. While every community and board are
always going to be a little different, there are some fundamental
principles that any board can take and apply. Boards and their
leadership modes and styles are different and will always be
changing due to the diversity of personalities on the board.
But rest assured of one thing: the power and ownership of any
nonprofit organization rests with the board. Although this part
of *The Perfect Nonprofit* Model may be an inexact science, it
needs much attention and focus.

The Three Types of Board Leadership

Three types of leadership models exist within any organization.
No matter who you are or how good or bad you think you are,
you will fall into or between one of these models. At the end of
the day, you want balance, shared responsibility, and trust.

Inverted Model

Executive dominates the board

The first model to examine is what we call an inverted model. In the inverted model, the board is led and informed by the agency executive of the organization. The executive is typically a type A, controlling person who has an innate desire to "run the show." He or she informs the board of the happenings within the organization and is typically making all of the vital decisions of the organization with little or no input from the board. In some circumstances, boards will "fall asleep at the wheel" and allow things to happen that could cause irreparable harm to the organization. A typical response from a board member who is a part of the inverted model might be, "Our executive is so strong that we do not have to worry about those types of decisions. Our executive will let us know when he/she needs our help. We just stay out of his way and let him/her make all of the decisions."

Micro-Management Model

Board dominates the executive

The micro-management model is the total opposite of the inverted model. In this model, the board is making every

62

decision of the organization, with little or no input from the organization's executive. In this model, the board could be making hiring decisions, deciding on delivery of programs, and making decisions on the day-to-day operations of the nonprofit. This model is equally as harmful as the inverted model because once again no checks and balances are in place to ensure that the organization is operating soundly. In addition, in most non-profits that employ people, the agency executive is looked upon by the community as a leader of the organization by default. If the executive is not empowered and allowed some levity to make day-to-day decisions, the organization will not be looked highly upon in its service area. A common phase stated by a board member in this model might be, "We are the decision-making body of the organization and we tell our executive what to do and when to do it. We do not want any hanky-panky or mismanagement on our watch. We watch every move being made down there."

Balanced Model

Board and executive roles are balanced

Once again, balance is the key to success, not only holistically, but from the board perspective. This nation was formed and has operated on balance of powers for over two centuries. Without a doubt, some of those framers of the balance of power had a hand in developing the structure that nonprofits are asked to govern by. With this in mind, balance of powers need to be clearly delineated between the board of directors and the executive. This will smooth out the waters of the organization and allow it to operate in an effective and efficient mode. Something you might hear from a board member who is serving in the balanced model might be, "We have trust within the board and the executive. That trust is built due to the checks and balances we have in place and we assure through those checks and balances that communication and transparency occur in a consistent and successful manner within our organization."

Obviously, we recommend the balanced model. If your organization falls in the Inverted or Micro-Management Models, or if you fall somewhere between those two and the Balanced Model, you need to begin to dialogue about how your organization can move towards the Balanced Model. How long it takes to get there will depend on how deeply your organization is immersed in the other two models.

Eight Key Functions of the Board

When it gets right down to it, a board has to function in an effective fashion for the organization to really be successful and meet the needs of its constituents. Everyone has their way of describing what board members should be doing individually and collectively to serve the mission and vision of the organization. Here is the problem that many boards face. At some time in the history of every nonprofit organization, the leadership needs to come to understand that you never quit learning. In addition, you are constantly looking for new and better ways to do what you do. This is a form of high-quality leadership that cannot be denied. Before I detail my eight key functions, let me tell you a story about board leadership.

The Perfect Example: No Organization Knows It All

I have been to more board meetings in my life than anyone close to my age. The majority of my meetings have been met by open arms and a keen enthusiasm to learn and grow. You know though,

5

there is always the exception to the rule. Recently, our company contracted with a nonprofit to consult with them on a resource development issue. Shortly after entering into the contract, we began to have issues. Members of the board were not happy with the approach we were taking in trying to consult with them. As a result, I agreed to travel to see the leadership of this organization onsite. As I began my presentation, which was just a precursor to the questions I anticipated would follow, I was stopped in my tracks by a man in the back of the room who proceeded to tell me that what I was presenting would not work in his community. He went as far to say that we should put an asterisk beside this organization because they were operating under extenuating circumstances. Another gentleman quickly told me that all of the supporters of this organization were tired and that we needed to focus on finding new donors that might be willing to give ten to fifteen dollars to the organization. Another lady lectured me about the fact the organization could raise seventy-five thousand dollars in small increments of twenty-five to one hundred dollars because her church had recently done it. (Author's note: Please be reminded this money raised by the church was raised in the same community that needed to have an asterisk placed beside it.) But wait, there's more! Part of my presentation was on prospecting new donors. The group was totally offended that we would consider prospecting anyone in the community for their giving potential. One lady went as far to assure we should be embarrassed about researching people and their private lives. It felt is if I'd been dropped behind the Iron Curtain. In one hour,

just sixty minutes, I was pretty much told that
we had no idea about resource development. In
that short time, I believe about eight covenants
of resource development were breached. Why did
this happen? How could a group of caring people
be so direct and set in their ways? Well, to me it
is really simple. At some place and time in the
history of this organization, they decided they had
a firm grasp on things and did not need anyone to
tell them how to conduct their business. They got
off the learning curve and are now paying dearly
for that decision. We were called in to help them
because they lost a significant income stream and
were not sure how to breach that gap.

This should serve as a reminder to all of us that when you feel
you know it all, you should probably move on to something
else. The best and brightest people I know are sponges. They are
constantly learning.

So what is the prescription for board success, individually and
collectively?

Board functions

Advocate! Advocate! Advocate!

Advocacy on behalf of a nonprofit organization is probably the easiest and most effective way you can help your organization. You simply have to brag to your friends and family about your organization. This may seem really simple to you, but fewer and fewer board members truly do this. When was the last time you talked about your organization to a group of fellow professionals? I am not talking about selling tickets or tables for a special event; I am talking about just telling your co-workers about what is happening in your organization. Tell your friends what a difference the organization is making in your community. Make sure that everyone knows that you are a member of the board for your organization. Very simply, using your name can provide your organization immeasurable market share. This brings me to share another experience that explains in my mind why advocacy is so important.

In our job, we often get to do confidential interviews to measure the validity of a proposed project. While conducting these interviews, we get to know the community and the organization more deeply than the most involved board member or constituent. As a part of this interview process, we ask questions about the leadership of the organization to the interviewee to assure the right leadership exists for the organization to be successful. A question we often ask is, "Can you name me one or more members of the board?" In more than one instance, we have had those interviewed say, "No, I do not know anyone on the board." Then the next step is to show the person being interviewed a board roster of the organization. Without fail, the person will look over the list and say, "Why, yes, I know several of these people. I did not know, however, they were serving on this board." This stands as a prime example that board members are not advocating on behalf of the organization.

Many board members may say they cannot advocate due to a

specific issue they are having with the organization. This could be an issue of a philosophical nature, or it may be a personal issue. If either of these exists, it is the responsibility of the individual board member to get in line with the program. If you cannot advocate on behalf of the organization, chances are you will not be successful at performing any other functions of the board at a desirable level.

Engage at a High Level

I have always wanted to ask, "If you are not sold on the organization, why are you serving on the board?" The reality is that the question is not easily answered. People feel compelled to serve nonprofit organizations at the board level for a myriad of reasons. In my time calling on boards, I have seen the entire spectrum of engagement. Some organizations are well aligned and have members engaged at a pretty high level. Other organizations have boards that are literally asleep at the wheel. These levels of engagement tend to be in direct correlation to the governance models mentioned earlier in this chapter. With this in mind, a board that is engaged can make wonderful things happen for the nonprofit.

I have often heard during my experiences working with a board, "It's the same six or seven people doing everything. We can't get anyone else to do a thing." This statement pretty much encompasses most boards. If you have read any literature about boards, or groups of any kind for that matter, the experts say 20 percent of the people do 80 percent of the work. Why does this happen? Well, I think there are a number of reasons for this phenomenon. The first reason is simple. If you are one of those who fall in the 20 percent category, you need to think about how to engage that other 80 percent at a higher level. You cannot be condescending about this either. Take into consideration what the 80 percent are thinking. Do you think they want to stand on the sideline? My guess is probably not. These board members who are in the 80 percent need to be strategically engaged and given a meaningful role within the organization.

If you are one of those 80 percent folks who do not do anything, find a niche in the organization and become more involved. It is difficult for those 20 percent board members to approach you because they are not certain where you stand on the work of the organization. In my mind, a great goal for every board member would be to get in that 20 percent group. Never, never stand on the sidelines as time goes by; you must engage. Remember one thing: if things go bad, you will be just as responsible for cleaning up the mess whether you are in the 20 percent group or 80 percent. So get involved and stay there.

Many times the work of an organization does not necessarily fit what some board members might sign on to do. In this case, as a board member it is incumbent to push yourself to do new things. In all reality, this is one of the opportunities that make board service so valuable. An example might be that you were recruited on the board due to your vast experience with legal issues facing nonprofits. The need of the organization might be to have people on the ground making face-to-face asks for an annual campaign. This being the case, you need to jump in there and make some face-to-face asks. Whatever the need, your involvement is vital to the nonprofit's success.

Knowing the mission of the organization for which you serve is also vital to your engagement. It amazes me how many board members serve and never really grasp the core reason for the existence of the organization. In the nonprofit world, mission and vision mean everything, which is why we devoted an entire chapter to this subject.

With all of this being said, organizations often place barriers to board member engagement without even knowing it. The list below cites examples of these barriers:

- Insufficient orientation

- The Board is too large

- The Board is too small

- The Executive Committee is too active

- Agendas are weak

- Members do not feel well-used or important

- There is little or no opportunity for discussion

- The board lacks social glue

Persevere Through the Good, the Bad and the Ugly

In the history of any organization, there will be times of crisis. Please understand this reality before you ever accept a position on a nonprofit board. Recently, I have noticed that when organizations experience crises, board members resign and run from the problems facing the organization. I believe this is a result of all of the mismanagement occurring in the for-profit world. Of course, this all resulted in Sarbanes-Oxley, which is legislation that affects the governance publicly-traded companies but also influences nonprofit governance. While this is all probably needed and will be good for governance in the long term, it is still incumbent on board members to show due-diligence in guiding their organizations out of crisis.

The true measure of a good nonprofit board is the way in which it guides an organization out of peril. This can also prove to be some of the most rewarding times of board service. You can actually make a difference in the organization. To understand all of this, you must understand and know that nonprofit management presents ebb and flow just as the corner drug store or local school district does in its history.

A true measure of a good board member is one who stays with the organization through the good times and the bad times. It is important for the health and welfare of the organization that board members dig in and provide the expertise to help the organization out of its woes. It is also important that board members conduct themselves with respect and dignity while managing crisis. Remember, eventually the skies will clear. You want to assure you can look each other in the face when the crisis ends. Walking through this process with an organization will make you appreciate the good times, while understanding and recognizing things could change very quickly.

Strategize for the Future

Charting the future of the organization is a vital function that every board member must take seriously. Many times this seems unimportant to board members, as they feel this should be the responsibility of others, but it is very clearly the responsibility of the board. In fact, it may be one of the most important things a board can do.

The Perfect Example: Any Road Will Lead There

I once was fortunate, a few years ago, to hear a young man give a speech to a large group of people. This young man was very unassuming. If you passed him on the street, you would not remember him. He was introduced to this group of people, probably in excess of 1,250, who were not remotely interested in him. He approached the podium and stated, "IF YOU DON'T KNOW WHERE YOU'RE GOING, ANY ROAD WILL LEAD YOU THERE." The crowd was silenced. He had their complete attention. He began to tell them how important it is for every individual and organization to chart their future. It goes without saying; this teenager received a standing ovation from the same crowd who ignored him in the beginning.

I tell this story because this young man made this large group think about the fact that any road can lead you there. Just think about the statement. It is profound. The young man went on to add that this statement was an ancient Chinese proverb. Now, telling this story as part of a book will not have the impact it did on those individuals assembled that evening but it sells the point that a path must be set for the future of your organization.

Strategic planning and its process were very popular several years ago. Well-intending people traveled across the country leading these planning meetings. They would capture the notes and then report back the findings with some objectives to get the organization to its ultimate goal in ten to fifteen years. These reports typically came in a decorative three-ring binder that gathered dust on the shelf of the executive.

Recently, we have come to understand that to get to that Envisioned Future organizations must have intermediate, tactical objectives to achieve in twelve to eighteen months. This seems to keep organizations involved in this process. Organizations that continue to plan are much more apt to be successful in about every facet of nonprofit management.

Charting the future of your organization, no matter how tedious, is important to you and your organization. If you are in a constant state of crisis, many nonprofit experts might suggest you wait to plan. I disagree. You may simply need a six- to twelve-month tactical plan that gets you out of crisis. Every organization worth its weight will have some type of plan in place that charts the future and lays forth a roadmap to get there. Strategy Development, as we call it, is covered in depth in the chapter on Mission and Vision.

5

Also please keep in mind that strategic plans come in all shapes and sizes. It does not matter how elaborate the plan is. It needs to be concise and aimed at your mission and vision, while having milestone objectives with a person or committee assigned the task. Lastly, this milestone should have a deadline for achievement set.

Remember, any road will lead you there!

Be Accountable to Yourself and Others

Accountability is huge in the nonprofit and for-profit world today. Obviously, it is always important. Being accountable for your actions as a board member can be the catalyst to drive the organization toward its mission and vision. As you serve on your board, there will times that issues will come forward that might affect you or your business directly. If this is the case, you must make certain that your actions are above any scrutiny. For example, if you are in the insurance business, obviously your organization will need some various types of coverage. Should you bid on the insurance? Should you serve on the committee that decides who gets the bid? These are difficult questions that need to be asked. What if you did write the insurance for the organization for which you serve? What would your response be when you were asked by other board members about your commission from the sale? What would your response be if other members of the board questioned the cost of the insurance? The example cited above touches on possible conflict of interest. The bottom line is, if you have the right people on the board, this will occur. Many organizations require all board members to sign a conflict of interest policy when joining the board. We strongly recommend that every organization institute this practice.

Board members must also assure they are apprised and updated on the health of the organization. One of the worst things that can happen to a board member is to be asked about something happening within the organization that they know nothing about. This is very embarrassing. Although it is the responsibility of the executive to communicate the organization's activities to the board, it is also the individual responsibility of each board member to be up to date on what is happening inside the organization. Lastly, if you do not understand part of what is happening within an organization, ask questions. Chances are other members of the board do not understand either.

Garner Resources in a Zealous Fashion

You cannot talk about board leadership without touching on the subject of raising money for your organization. Fund development seems to always be the part of an organization that gives members of the board the most angst. Very simply, it seems that most board members have trouble soliciting money for the cause. It is my belief that the reason for this dilemma runs deeper than just fear. If a board member is sold and committed to the mission and vision of the organization, they will not be so apprehensive to ask for money. I also believe that if a board member is completely comfortable with the operations of the organization, they will be more likely to make an ask. Getting to this point is the problem. While an organization is progressing, it is sometimes difficult to get all board members to agree they are happy with what is happening with the organization. This is why it is supremely important for an organization to have a plan and goals to work toward. Equally important is the fact the board needs to be committed to the mission and vision of the organization. If board members are focused on the future, mission, and vision they will not worry so much about the present. This will occur because they will be able to sell the future of the organization.

In closing, it is the responsibility of every member of the board to raise the resources necessary to sustain the organization. If you are uncomfortable with this, there are strategies available that will help you get through this fear. Also remember, this is not an uncommon feeling for a board member to experience. So hang in there until you read about a more detailed strategy on how to effectively raise funds later in the book.

5

Set Governance Structure that Builds Public Trust

Every nonprofit has a governance structure. What type of structure you implement is up to you as a board. Please let me give you one word of caution. If you do not build trust in your community, you will have trouble functioning as an organization. This can be avoided by advocating a few things the organization should adopt as common practice.

First, you need to give surety that the organization has sound financial policies and procedures that guarantee the organization operates in a fashion that is not only acceptable to, but embraced by the community that is charged with supporting it. This may sound simple, but nonprofits tend to struggle with this from time to time. Sound financial policies and procedures are readily available. As a matter of fact, your CPA can provide a set that will be more than acceptable.

Next, make sure the organization is in compliance with all local, state, and federal statutes and laws. These tend to change on a regular basis, so you need to assure you retain adequate legal counsel to keep you and the organization aware of the law. Nothing can be more disconcerting than to get the organization in trouble because of a new law or statute.

Lastly, it is the responsibility of the board to oversee all of this. You as a board member must monitor all of the progress in reference to this. Learn more about this responsibility in the governance chapter of the book.

Provide Leadership and Insight

Boards and those who serve on them are meant to provide guidance and leadership to the organization. This can sometimes be difficult due to others and their leadership styles, or lack thereof in most cases. Providing leadership and insight to the organization requires each board member to act on their responsibility as a trustee of the organization. You can be a great leader to the organization by assuring that you are clear and up to date on what is occurring within the organization. It is almost impossible for you as a leader to provide insight that is of a positive nature if you are not apprised of the dealings of the organization.

Board Leadership - the Inexact Science

It is important in your time of service to find out where your leadership style fits within the organization. Obviously those leading the organization at the board level officers and those in command will have the most influence when it comes to leadership. It is the responsibility of all board members to assure the organization is led in an adequate and accurate fashion. Providing quality leadership is a very difficult task in the nonprofit and for-profit worlds, and finding folks willing to lead is more difficult than ever.

Why is leadership with boards and organizations somewhat difficult to define? It is the charge of every board member and board body to assure the organization is not put in peril due to a lack of leadership. In today's world with all the malfeasance and all the negativity heaped upon for-profit and nonprofit organizations, it is difficult not only to find people who will lead but to find those individuals who will lead with great humility and courage. While this is a very difficult time for leaders, it is imperative, particularly in the nonprofit world, that organizations have this leadership infused so it drives the organization as well as its vision and mission. While this may not seem important, it is more vital than you could ever imagine. When organizations are not led, they will move in any

76

particular direction, which means, as illustrated in this book, organizations will not follow their mission and the vision. And as you know, when an organization, particularly a nonprofit, does not follow its mission and its vision, the result will be negative.

Margaret Mead once said, "Never doubt that a small group of committed citizens can change the world. Indeed it is the only thing that ever has." The reality of the situation is that you've read it many times because it in fact sums up board service. Equally, when you decide as an individual board member that you are truly committed to the cause of the organization that you serve, you will truly work miracles within it.

Your leadership and insight as a board member will only be as strong as your dedication to the mission and the vision of the organization. Many great leaders have come and gone. We read about them in all types of books and periodicals. Yet they all have one thing in common: they rose to the occasion when it was demanded of them and fought for what they thought was right and did what they thought was right for their organization or entity. In layman's terms, this describes nonprofit board service and leadership. Board members must provide for the organization to be truly successful and then drive the mission and vision to its successful end.

Leadership styles and personalities will affect the way you as an individual board member can lead and provide insight to the organization. Many people who serve on boards allow this to be a barrier to their service in leadership. An example I cite would be personalities. In many cases, as human beings, we will not allow our personalities to get out of the way of success. Many great things that could have been done in the nonprofit sector and the for-profit sector have never happened because human beings could not get over the personalities and the likes and dislikes that those personalities bring to bear. In my experience working with and on nonprofit boards, this has been the paramount issue that all boards at some time face. It is my recommendation that each and every board, no matter how big or small, conduct personality profile tests of each individual board member and executive professional. Once these personality profiles are completed, the organization can then begin to assess what its entire organizational personality looks like. Knowing this would allow for good decisions and no frustration with one another when difficult times arise. This may seem somewhat elementary to some of you, but I have seen as many organizations falter at this juncture in their history as I have seen succeed. This is why I strongly recommend that each organization take its own personality profile test. We at *The Perfect Nonprofit* do not endorse any particular personality test although there are many good examples for you to investigate. My experience with the personality profiles is that whichever one you choose to take, it will help you understand how your organization interacts and how you will want to conduct its business. This is an irrefutable aspect of leadership and insight of a board. Again, it may seem somewhat elementary to some but it is one of the most important functions you can perform to help move your organization forward while enlightening and enhancing your service on your nonprofit board.

It is my belief that many of the roles board members play in the life of a nonprofit are in fact counterintuitive. This makes it difficult at times for boards to work together. Time and time again, successful leaders are generally successful because they are intuitive. This is also the case in nonprofit management with a few exceptions. I mention this only because at times a board member's decisions are not based on intuitive thought but rather counterintuitive thought. While one of my goals in writing this book is not to be academic, I want to ensure that *The Perfect Nonprofit* Model leaves no stone unturned in communicating what we feel works best in the board room. An example of counterintuitive decision making could be in the board dealing with its executive. If you feel board service is somewhat difficult, put yourself in the seat of the nonprofit executive. Imagine how you would feel if you had a new boss every year or two. Envision working for a community-based organization in which thirty-five people who served on the board feel they are your supervisor. Herein lies the job of the agency executive. As board members, you hold the collective fate of the agency executive in your hand. One of the primary functions of the board is to hire, maintain, and fire the nonprofit executive if needed. When making these types of decisions, it is important for a board member to assure that there is no stone unturned. In relation to the executive, whether the board is hiring or dismissing, this is one of the most important functions that can be served.

I present you with a unique thought in closing. Sometimes the most important things in life we must address are given the least amount of credence. If charitable and nonprofit organizations were not led by effective, well-meaning, mission-driven board members, where would the future of this country be? Recently I heard a gentleman make a statement about nonprofits and charities. He stated, "Charitable organizations give citizens in the community an opportunity to stand for what they believe and help others who need it the most, all while giving back. This in turn, gives us the opportunity to feel good about something in this country." In my mind, this sums up why boards are important and why board service is one of the key cogs in *The Perfect Nonprofit* model.

I have stated throughout this chapter many of the reasons organizations struggle or succeed from the board perspective. Cited below are some of the reasons why boards are not successful. They may seem simple, but many times they derail organizations. Take some time and look over these reasons cited below and ask yourself, "Where do you and your organization fall?"

- No communication within the organization

- Poor group dynamic

- Lack of organizational knowledge

- No balance of power within the organization

- Lack of pride and belief in the mission and/or the organization

- No sense of the future and what it holds

- Apathy

- Tenure or lack of tenure

- Acceptance and adherence to the 80/20 rule

After reading this you may ask yourself, will I ever be able to be successful as a board member? The answer to the question is "Yes." All board service can be difficult at times; it can be some of the most rewarding work you will ever do. Organizations that have successful boards tend to work at it on a daily and monthly basis. In retrospect, board service is like anything else in this world. If you are willing to work at it, be the best you can be so the entire organization will benefit from your efforts. It just takes time and effort on your part and the part of your organization. The reality of the situation is if this is not a priority within your organization, you will never reach the heights of success that you dream of nor will the mission and vision of your organization ever be realized to its full extent. It is my hope that you all dream of being *The Perfect Nonprofit*. If this is your dream, then it begins with the Board of Directors.

Further information, tools, and services are available at www.theperfectnonprofit.com

Governance - the Foundation of Achievement

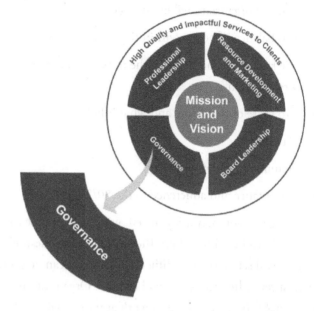

The entire concept of creating a governance model for a nonprofit agency revolves around one key component: developing a TEAM. Perhaps the single-most important component of identifying and implementing a governance model is getting each and every member of the board and executive staff to have ownership of the process and to understand that no one person can dominate the organization or push forward a personal agenda if it is to succeed. Most nonprofit organizations choose a traditional governance model where there is a Board of Directors, which by definition has a primary role of setting policy and raising money. This board then employs an executive professional who builds the administrative team and is charged with administering the policies set by the board and expends the money the board raises within the parameters of the set budget, which in itself is a policy statement.

In this chapter of *The Perfect Nonprofit*, we will explore how to build and instill the TEAM concept in your organization, evaluate a three-tier governance model, talk about the fundamental knowledge of nonprofit finance, and finally discuss the basic understanding of the legal duties of the board and the organization.

Developing the TEAM That Will Carry You to Success

Definition of team: Two or more people who work interdependently and adaptively toward a common goal, have specific roles, function over a limited time span, and have a team goal versus an individual goal.

What makes a team effective is the belief in the cause; have confidence and precise execution of the game plan. In order to be an effective team there must be a high level of interdependence among team members while the team leader must have good people skills and be committed to the team approach. Each team member must be willing to contribute to the team process and the team must develop a relaxed climate for communication. Team members need to develop a mutual trust of each other and each individual must be prepared to take risks. The team must be clear about its goals and objectives. They also must be willing and able to establish focused targets in order to succeed. Each and every team member must have their role clearly defined and there needs to be assurances that they understand and support it. They must know how to examine both team and individual errors, but without making personal attacks on the source of the error. Team members should feel they have both the capacity and the ability to create and bring new ideas to the team without feeling they will be dismissed without fair hearing. Most importantly, each team member needs to know he or she can influence the team's agenda.

You can have the best team in the world but without an effective game plan you will not win the game. The game plan establishes the focus of the organization and serves as the basis for all decision making relative to every aspect of the organization's strategic initiative.

6 A Different Governance Model for Different Times

As stated earlier in this chapter, most nonprofits have adopted the traditional governance solely driven by one body, the Board of Directors, with standing committees. Please see the organizational chart below as an example of this model.

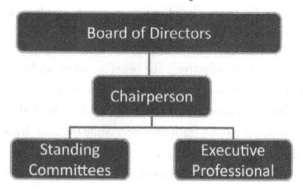

Traditional Board Model

While this model works, the case could be made that it fails to capitalize on the myriad number of volunteers and supporters who would like to participate with your agency but do not have the time or inclination to dedicate the hours needed to either serve on a board or assume the responsibility that comes with such membership. They will, however, give you some time and in other cases will provide significant support as long as it does not require them to commit large blocks of time. To fully enlist all of these various types of investors, donors, and those who want to actively participate in the leadership of the organization requires a multi-tier approach to your governance model.

First let me state that there was, is, and always will be a need for an active, engaged, committed, and dedicated Board of Directors for any agency that truly wishes to succeed at the highest level. However, in many cases this singular approach to governance can no longer sustain the work of the organization and the multiplicity of needs that present themselves in the nonprofit landscape. An active board oversees the setting of policy, the raising of money and fulfills all of the oversight and fiduciary needs of the organization. This is the heart and soul of the governance model. There is another group, however, that gathers on occasion to help the organization. This group may get together once or twice a year but when needed rises to the occasion with their checkbook in hand to provide immediate relief in times of distress or provide the necessary funding to take the organization to the next level. Some organizations refer to this group as life members, trustees, governors, etc. What they are in fact are true believers in your cause who choose to support you but who cannot or will not participate on a weekly or monthly basis. This group along with the Board of Directors provides two tiers of governance.

The final tier is a group of people who are almost always overlooked by the nonprofit world. This group is comprised of people who may be on their way up in the corporate world, who are community activists, who believe in the concept of volunteerism, and who wish to make a difference in their community. This group can range in number from a few dedicated event volunteers to vast groups of over one hundred people or more. Their common bond is their willingness to work on your behalf without having to participate in monthly meetings. They become a vast pool of volunteers for all of your events, sales, and solicitations. Known by many names, this group has been called Board of Corporators (a term often used by hospitals), advisory boards, unit boards, and a host of other names that collectively describe this totally volunteer-oriented group. Some organizations using this model charge modest annual dues to make sure those involved are committed to the process. They are almost always invited to the annual meeting of the Board of Directors to hear of the work the agency is doing and what role is planned for them in the coming year. Some

6

organizations actually run social events throughout the year to keep the group together and focused while providing them with a social outlet. Regardless of what they are called and how they are structured, this group can and does make a huge difference in those organizations who adopt this model. In some cases, organizations use this group like a farm system in major league baseball to feed the full Board of Directors. Once they have proven themselves on the volunteer board, they are groomed to someday take a place on the Board of Directors.

This three-tier system or variations thereof does not cost the organization any extra money to implement. On the contrary, if designed and executed effectively this model can and does have a tremendously positive impact on the financial well being of the organization. From the annual significant contributions of the Board of Trustees, to the efforts in raising resources on the Board of Directors, the countless volunteers who serve as the advisory board each one brings a unique benefit to the organization. This benefit will not only help your organization in the short term but will provide you with the ability to develop long-range planning that will help you address your future needs and to help prepare you for what may lie ahead.

While this model, which we recommend, provides even further balance and equilibrium to your organization that is the primary concept upon which *The Perfect Nonprofit* is built, there are other models that can provide an equal measure of innovation to your organization. No matter what model you choose, you need to realize that you are not limited by the traditional approach to board/staff governance. Your only limitation is your imagination and the willingness of your Board of Directors to try something new and different. You are only limited by your own creativity and imagination. There is no right or wrong model. Whatever model works for you and meets the needs of your organization is the right one.

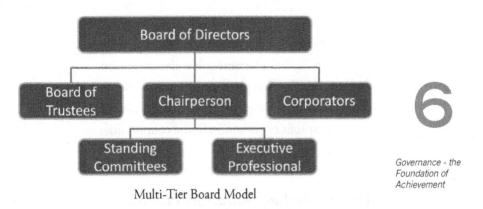

Multi-Tier Board Model

The Perfect Example: Three Tiers Hurrah!

One of the most effective uses of this three-tier model has been used for the past thirty years by a nonprofit youth organization that has seen significant success over the past thirty years. Utilizing a Board of Trustees, Board of Directors, and Board of Corporators approach in their governance model, this organization holds their annual meeting during the month of December each year. They hold their meeting in a local restaurant and their attendance is always in the 100 to 150 range. The annual meeting of the Board of Directors is held, the annual meeting of the Board of Trustees is held, and the election of new officers for each is held along with the election of new Corporators and the renewal of those whose terms may be ending. This meeting serves as the focal point for the entire year and is the only time all three boards are ever in the same place. This organization over good times and bad, through economic boom times and busts, and during times of stability and great growth, has always maintained its balance and equilibrium. They have always raised money, always run successful events, and have never wanted for effective volunteers. Finally, they always know where their next generation of leadership is coming from because it has already proven itself. They have perfected this three-tier model and because they have, they are the dominant nonprofit organization in the communities in which they serve.

Understanding Nonprofit Finance

The Nonprofit Paradigm

The entire concept behind *The Perfect Nonprofit* is to create an equilibrium or balance in the various components of nonprofit management, governance, and resource development. Balance virtually guarantees a well-grounded organization that will constantly be challenging itself and its supporters to continually move the agency forward. Therefore, it is only logical that the paradigm used in the generation of financial resources also be equally balanced and in a state of equilibrium. Too many organizations become dependent on one source of revenue or another based on expediency and comfort giving little thought to what might happen to the organization if for some reason that primary source of funding were to disappear. Unfortunately, in all our years working with nonprofits, the over reliance on one source of revenue tends to be the norm and the not the exception. While we can cite numerous examples of this, perhaps the best way to illustrate this for the reader is to compare the following charts. These percentages are taken from actual case studies of nonprofit organizations from around the country. Some of them were able to adapt and are thriving today. Some of them never adapted and are no longer with us and the shame in that is the people they were helping are no longer receiving vital services.

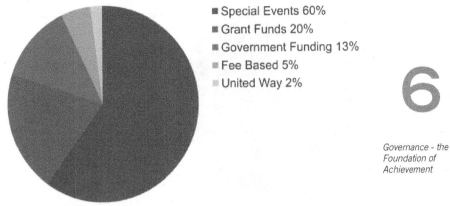

- Special Events 60%
- Grant Funds 20%
- Government Funding 13%
- Fee Based 5%
- United Way 2%

Governance - the Foundation of Achievement

Imbalanced Funding: Dominated by Special Events

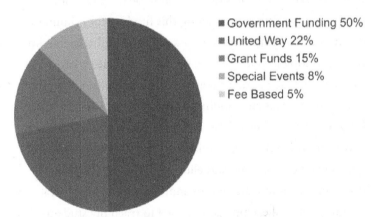

- Government Funding 50%
- United Way 22%
- Grant Funds 15%
- Special Events 8%
- Fee Based 5%

Imbalanced Funding: Dominated by Government

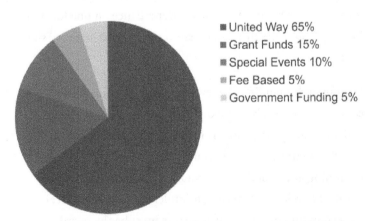

- United Way 65%
- Grant Funds 15%
- Special Events 10%
- Fee Based 5%
- Government Funding 5%

Imbalanced Funding: Dominated by United Way

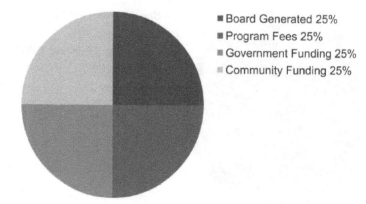

- Board Generated 25%
- Program Fees 25%
- Government Funding 25%
- Community Funding 25%

Balanced funding Funding

It would serve you as an organization to be truly introspective in evaluating where you fall along this funding continuum to determine both your organization's strengths and vulnerabilities. It is interesting to note that the agency that ceased to exist was the one that was dependent on government funding. The reason for this was an inability to anticipate a downturn in this funding. Unlike United Way and Special Event funding that may diminish over time, in this case the government funding was in place one day and was eliminated during the change from one city administration to another with no clear advanced warning. As a college professor, I used to teach my students that an issue only becomes a problem when you fail to deal with it as an issue and a problem only becomes a crisis when it is not solved as a problem. The issue of over reliance on one form of funding is an issue that can blossom into a crisis in a very short time.

In fully understanding the revenue side of the financial equation, it must also be stated that the Board of Directors and any and all other boards in the governance model you choose must also understand the concept of "Charity Beginning at Home." It is imperative that whatever type of resource development plan you implement there be a clear understanding that the first investors must be the board members and volunteers that populate your governance model.

This is not an option. Anyone associated with organization and functioning within the governance model must make a meaningful financial contribution to the organization or evaluate why they have chosen to serve. There is an old adage that states there is no such thing as an absolute. The individual who coined this phrase did not understand nonprofit resource development support from the board and volunteers.

6

Many questions need to be asked by board members in relation to revenue generation. In addition, board members must gain an understanding of the revenue-generating arm of a nonprofit. Does one source of funding for your organization exceed 50 percent of you revenue? This is the proverbial *sword of Damocles* just waiting to lop off the head of your organization. Just take a minute to calculate what you would have to do to overcome an immediate 50 percent reduction in your revenue stream should you lose this funding. Short of have an angel showing up with a check (which we assume would be cashable), most nonprofits could not survive this disaster. A second and equally important question is, "Does your nonprofit rely on a source of funding that is cyclical?" While not as damaging as our first example, this aspect of funding is contingent on making sure your application is in on time and also that you continue to meet the requirements of the investor. Another factor here is sensitivity to a downturn in the economy that can in fact change the availability of the funds even if you have been a regular recipient. The final question asks, "Does your organization base its operations on generating revenues that are subject to conditions beyond your control?" This becomes an acute problem when these funds are linked to government approval, private foundations, or other groups where you are at the mercy of their current circumstance, board of directors, or requirements for continued funding.

6

*Governance - the
Foundation of
Achievement*

Understanding the Expense Side

Like the understanding of your revenue streams, there are key questions that must be answered relative to the methods in which your organization expends its resources, "Does your organization operate on a balanced budget?" Economic stability is like a double-edge sword. You need a stable budget to instill confidence in the investors of your organization to raise the necessary funding to meet your operational needs. However, the nonprofits most in need of this support do not have stable budgets. It is like the old story of the only time a bank wants to lend you money is when you don't need it. Of equal importance is to comprehend the breakdown of the expense components of your organization. What is the percentage breakdown of your administrative costs vs. salaries and benefits for direct service staff? What is the percentage of your overall program costs? How much do you spend on facilities, maintenance, and operations? A critical question that must be addressed is, "Does your organization carry any debt service?" The answer to this last question can determine to a great extent the ability to raise money from investors in that having to borrow money carries with it an implied inability to manage the money you have been raising. The final analysis is how these costs compare with other agencies your size in your particular market area. The Board of Directors must clearly understand how the accounting for the organization is handled and needs to be fully cognizant of any issues around the items discussed above.

As a Board of Directors, you are obligated to both understand the current financial position of your nonprofit and ask questions when things do not appear to be correct. As board members you are charged with the ultimate responsibility for the financial well being of the organization and you need to have all of the information at your fingertips. Accountability and transparency, which are the decade's catch phrases, are even more important in terms of the board's understanding of the agency than they are for potential investors.

Legal Duties of the Board and Organization

There are three fundamental areas of legal duties of any member of a nonprofit board of directors: the duty of care, loyalty, and obedience. Each of these three areas has specific responsibilities and duties and together comprises the code of ethics for a nonprofit board and a prescriptive analysis of what is expected both legally and morally.

Performance of the duty of care involves the board members intimate knowledge of the mission, planning, and policies and ensure that they in every way meet not only the needs of the population being served but also meet the needs of the community in which the programs and services are executed. Board members must be cognizant of the charter, by-laws, and general statutes that govern the nonprofit organization for which they served. They must ensure that any and all decisions they make not only conform to the letter of the laws but also to the needs of the community they serve. These last tenets revolve around the duty of obedience. This is relevant to not only the collective conscience of the agency and its board but to the legislative regulations that apply to each and every nonprofit organization.

When accepting members on a Board of Directors, each director should understand clearly that they are agreeing to fully participate in the organization in terms of attendance at board meetings, participation in open discussion, and in the decision-making process that will guide the organization in everything it does. Many people agree to serve on a volunteer Board of Directors not out of a sense of service but because of the person who asks them or they think it will look good on their resume. This is not only a disservice to the organization but to the other members of the board who fully understand that they are obligated to not only participate in a meaningful way but to also read any and all documents pertaining to the governance of the agency including minutes of meetings, financial reports, job performance evaluations, and accreditation reports should they be applicable to their particular agency.

6

Of even greater importance is a point that has been driven home throughout this entire chapter and the one on Resource Development and Marketing. Each board member has a fiduciary responsibility to ensure the organization has sufficient resources, which includes people, funding, assets, and staff to adequately deliver the programs and services they offer at the highest level possible.

In terms of the duty of loyalty, it is the specific responsibility of each board member to focus on establishing priorities for their nonprofit organization and to ensure that they do not put their personal agenda or that of another agency ahead of the organization on whose board they serve. Participation on a nonprofit board not only implies that the board member will share their energy, intellect, and monetary resources with the agency but that they actually do so. One of the most critical legal duties of the board is to select and retain the professional executive of the agency, provide them with a detailed job description, establish mutually agreeable goals, and then evaluate the executive fairly in relation to the attainment of these goals. In terms of their responsibility to the remainder of the professional staff, the board serves as the final arbiter of grievances that may come about as a result of the progressive employee disciplinary system that should be in place for every nonprofit agency.

The board should continually analyze their own individual performance through self-evaluation as well as assessing the performance of the overall board. This can be accomplished through periodic review of the board's goals and objectives and have a specific report card annually to ensure they are meeting the basic criteria of board membership for their specific agency. The concept of the board contract often discussed by many agencies but rarely implemented is one way to ensure adherence to the basic responsibilities of each board member to the agency.

The board must adhere to the fundamental tenets of its own charter and by-laws by ensuring that each meeting has a quorum of members to ensure that all actions taken at the meeting are both binding and legal. Boards that consistently have trouble attaining a quorum need to start the evaluation process for determining if, in fact, they have the right membership. Board members need to know that they have legal liabilities that come with their membership and have the right to know that the organization is carrying Board of Directors insurance and that it is always in good standing. Service to a nonprofit board should be both enjoyable and rewarding. Knowing your legal rights helps to ensure that this is not only possible but certain.

Conclusion

The focus of this chapter has centered on the governance of a nonprofit organization from the point of view of the board member. *The Perfect Nonprofit* Model is designed to create a balanced approach to every aspect of nonprofit management, governance, resource development, marketing, and service delivery. A key component of this is the necessary knowledge each board member must have regarding the financial and legal aspects, their board membership, as well as the governance model the agency chooses to use to maximize their impact in the community they serve. Governance is more than knowing the law and going to meetings, it is internalizing each and every aspect of board involvement, developing a knowledge base on which to support their participation, and having the necessary information to maximize their impact on the board.

Further information, tools, and services are available at www.theperfectnonprofit.com

Quality and Impactful Services to Clients - Begin with the End

Quality and Impactful Services to Clients - Begin with the End

Service Delivery

Perhaps no other area in the holistic model that is *The Perfect Nonprofit* is more important than the area of service delivery. Regardless of your mission, if you do not deliver the services promised in that Mission Statement, there is no reason for your organization to exist. You can have a mesmerizing board, dynamic professional leadership, and have a fundraising machine, but if you are not meeting a real need in your community and delivering your programs and services at the highest level to meet that need then your organization is just a sham. You might ask if there are nonprofits that operate this way and, unfortunately, the answer is, "Yes."

Community Assessment

Identifying the Need

The critical element in determining your service delivery model is obviously identifying and validating the need within the community that you serve. While this can be done in a number of ways, the single-best way to determine the need, evaluate organizations that are already addressing these needs, evaluate how successful they are in meeting these needs, identify areas that still need to be addressed, and develop a service delivery model to address these underserved areas is a full community assessment. The concept of the community assessment is predicated on both collecting demographic information along with actual input from current and future stakeholders to ensure that the needs you have identified to address are real and priorities for your community. In addition, the assessment can direct you in determining the design of the best model to deliver the programs and services needed to address the issues identified.

The online research component makes extensive use of the myriad search engines on the web that both identify and quantify the demographic profile of your community. It provides the statistical validation of the need you are addressing in your mission. A primary example would be you have to know how many homeless people there are in your community if you are proposing opening a homeless shelter. While this seems like an overly simplistic example, it is taken from reality. We were once contacted by a group who was preparing to open a homeless shelter only to find out after the community assessment that there were virtually no homeless people in the community. While it had an occasional transient population that could be construed as being homeless, the fact remained that the population and the need that the agency sought to help did not exist to any great measure, thus making their objective superfluous. While examples like this, fortunately, are few and far between, the fact remains that for every need in a given community there are often multiple agencies trying to address it. The larger the community, the greater the need, and the more agencies there are competing with one another to address it.

Quality and Impactful Services to Clients - Begin with the End

7

Identification of Key Leadership and Philanthropic Centers

Using a comprehensive system of online research, individual interviews, and focus groups, the community assessment process provides the concrete foundation for constructing not only the service delivery model but also for identifying the key philanthropic centers in your community that are potential supporters for the nonprofit and its cause. A comprehensive community assessment can also play a dominant role in identifying potential key board members and supporters. For the assessment to be successful, it should have a component dedicated to analyzing the corporate, foundation, and philanthropic community. This analysis should include overall giving, community involvement, the focus of their current giving, and whether they support the conceptual focus of the programs and services you are currently providing or hope to provide. The reality of the current nonprofit world is that there is overwhelming competition for the same investor dollars. It is critical that your organization have the necessary market research to determine what your market share should be and identify the potential investors that you need to target. You will also need to know where there current support is being focused and, in fact, if you can compete successfully to get your share.

Collaboration and Partnership

Another focal point in the execution of a comprehensive community assessment is identifying potential organizations or agencies for possible collaboration and/or partnership. The nonprofit world is changing dramatically and rapidly. Many investors, both individual and foundations, will not even consider investing their money in organizations that are not collaborating or partnering with each other to provide proactive services in a cost-effective service model that not only addresses the need identified in the mission but maximizes the impact of their investment. Impact, outcome measurement, and validating results are the keys to securing support. Doing this in the context of a meaningful partnership is a further demonstration to the investor community that you are serious about what you do and are prudent stewards of their investments.

Using the Results

The end result of the community assessment is not only the generation of an in-depth report but the creation of a roadmap that will provide your organization with the necessary information to make informed decisions relative to future growth. The depth and specificity of the data provided becomes the necessary foundation to evaluate the choices you are faced with as you seek to move your organization to the next level. However, a report is only as good as its implementation plan. Many nonprofit organizations have invested money in executing a community assessment only to ignore the findings of the report. The final report will provide you with strong support for your initial hypothesis; however, the results of the report are not written from the perspective of what you want to hear but rather from what you need to hear. It is not uncommon for the results of such an assessment to refute the thinking of the organization and provide it with input that would send it in a different direction. This is the purpose of the process. A comprehensive community assessment is meant to validate your mission, refine your current service delivery model, and provide you with the information you need to secure more funding. In addition, it could provide you with evidence you are moving in the wrong direction, need to create a new service delivery model, and change the culture of your organization to consider new ways to partner and collaborate. This could result in allowing your organization to target a whole new class of donor. While it takes courage and foresight to undertake such an assessment, it takes even more courage and a dedication of purpose to take the results provided and implement them to change the focus and course of your organization.

Quality and Impactful Services to Clients - Begin with the End

7

Quality and Impactful Services to Clients - Begin with the End

- Defines and validates the need you are hoping to address in your mission statement

- Provides the necessary demographic statistics to quantify this validation

- Taps the collective thinking of individuals and focus groups to further support your organization's focus

- Identifies and qualifies future board members

- Identifies, qualifies, and evaluates future investors

- Identifies and evaluates competing agencies who are seeking to address the same or similar needs

- Creates a focal point for determining your market share of the investor pool

- Identifies potential collaborations and partnerships that can change the culture of the organization and result in streamlining operations and maximizing the cost effectiveness of your service delivery model

- Provides your agency with the necessary information on which to make informed decisions about future growth

- Provides you with a roadmap to success

Defining Your Impact

The information provided in the community assessment provides how you define and deliver your programs and services. Upon receipt of the final report of your community assessment, the information needs to be shared with the current board and executive leadership staff to be used in devising a master plan to either bolster your current service delivery model and adjust, and yes maybe even replace, it in order to maximize your impact in the community. The entire being of a nonprofit organization needs to be the impact it is having in executing its mission and the resulting impact it has on improving the quality of life for the community-at-large.

Keep in mind without the information you have uncovered in the community assessment, you are only guessing at whether or not you are actually meeting the needs of the community or even more importantly, if the community perceives you are meeting its needs. From the actual location of your facilities, to the programs and services you offer, to the service population you are serving, all that you are and hope to be resolves around the simple equation of how you are impacting the community in meeting the needs in your mission and does that community agree with that perception. There is an old adage that "Perception is Reality." This concept is absolutely true when it comes to the perceived impact a nonprofit is having on the communities in which they serve. We all know of organizations by virtue of national affiliation or reputation enjoys an incredibly strong perception of community impact, while other smaller and less well-known organizations may not have this perception. Equally, we also know that many times this community perception is not warranted and that the smaller, more focused agency is, in actuality, having a greater impact. Some would decry this as injustice and that it is unfair, and it is. However, the one ultimate definer of community impact is statistical evaluation, definitive outcome measurement, supported data, and a myriad of other irrefutable documentation that not only implies your success, but proves it.

It is the proof of your impact that becomes a motivator in targeting and recruiting stronger boards, larger investors, better staff, and increasing your community reputation so that it is your nonprofit whose name comes to mind whenever the discussion turns to your service population. As nonprofit organizations traverse the dangerous waters of this century more and more, the reefs that lie in wait to wreck their ships are the inability to clearly demonstrate their outcomes and impact. Increasing numbers of foundations and, in particular, social entrepreneurs, are not only looking for the outcomes you are

7

achieving, they are demanding them. Those agencies that have
ridden the coattails of national organization marketing now
have to clearly demonstrate their specific impact and outcomes.
Likewise, those smaller organizations can distinguish themselves
as the playing field is leveled through the reporting of specific
community impact and outcomes. The ultimate test is that the
setting of goals and objectives for every aspect of the nonprofit
spectrum now become mandatory because you cannot measure
where you are when you have not set a goal of where you
wanted to be. Measurement is specific, democratic, and focused.
It does not require interpretation, only validation. The process
of setting goals and objectives for your organization starts with
the specific intelligence and analysis you receive in the results
of your assessment. This then translates into timed, measurable,
and assigned objectives that can be measured using a specific
schedule. These goals and objectives have also defined methods
to measure their attainment, which is spelled out in detail at the
beginning of the process. Finally, the result of that measurement
generated by the methods adopted becomes irrefutable evidence
that what you are doing works. The benefit is that it is not
you tooting your own horn; it is a statistical validation of your
results. An added benefit is that they can be monitored monthly
and be revised if they are not working.

This management by objective system starts with having the
necessary knowledge to create attainable and meaningful goals
while having a service delivery model that is defined by specific
objectives to attain these goals. The confidence it builds within
the staff and more importantly, the Board of Directors, is
the glue that holds it together. This model has existed in the
business world forever and it has proven successful time and
again. One of the critical issues nonprofits face is that they do
not seek to govern their organizations or provide their product,
programs and services with the same focused, targeted approach
needed for their business. The concept of nonprofit is only
that. Some people use it as an excuse to apply poor business

thinking and/or practices. The reality is that your organization is a business. It generates revenues, has products (your programs and services), and more importantly, it needs to report to its stockholders (the people who invest in you). Call it what you want, but you are a business; the only difference is that your profit margin is the impact you are having in your community and any excess revenues get immediately reinvested in the products.

Quality and Impactful Services to Clients - Begin with the End

Communicating Your Impact

The ability to take all that we have discussed, develop a comprehensive reporting process, and communicate your impact to the community becomes the foundation for all future success. The interesting thing is that in constructing your message of positive impact, the best people to use are those who are benefitting directly — your service population. You should absolutely have an annual report that looks more like a corporate annual report than a feel good piece extolling your virtues. You need to start thinking in terms of the kinds of presentations you make to civic groups, support networks, and yes, even your clients. The impact you are achieving needs to be not only quantified and validated but reported in the context of the humanity you are working with. Focus on the service population, your service delivery model, its cost effectiveness, and its return on investment will set you apart from your competitors who want to focus their results on human interest alone. We are not saying to abandon the human interest aspect of communicating your impact. Emotion and passion most certainly have their place in your impact and outcomes. What we are saying is that you had better be able to quantify, validate, and prove your impact and outcomes within the context of those human interest stories if you want to succeed at the highest level and instill confidence in your board, staff, clients, and most importantly, your investors.

102

The Perfect Example: The Report to the Stockholders

A nonprofit organization that we worked with decided to change the way they constructed their annual fundraising strategy. Instead of doing the tried and true annual campaign, they decided to sell stock in the organization. This is not being reported here because it was a wildly successful fundraiser, which it was. It is being reported here because this organization decided in order to take this concept to the next level; they needed to make an annual report to their stockholders. To do this they decided to abandon their usual annual report and in its place develop a corporate report to the stockholders. This report highlighted the return on investment to those people who purchased stock in the organization. The report featured vast improvement organizational programs and services. With each passing year, the results have been more astounding with greater numbers of shares being bought by individuals and businesses. Further, the return on their investment has continued to soar thus not only making their investment worthwhile but making a preferred stock in the minds of many. More importantly, the organization's annual report is positive proof that what they are doing works and warrants the support of the investors who have chosen to buy the stock.

Description of Service Delivery Models

In defining your organization's service delivery model, the one thing you should remember is that there is no standard, perfect delivery model. Rather, the profile of your service delivery model should be based on several key questions that you can analyze as you devise your model. You should also keep in mind that many local nonprofit organizations that are an affiliated with a national organization may have a service delivery model defined for them. These national models, however, should also be made to stand the test of the same key questions you must answer honestly in defining your local model.

The first question that your organization must ask in defining your service delivery model is, "Do our programs and services address the needs of the community as defined by the community?" In many cases, when you analyze why a nonprofit is failing, it is because they have not been responsive to focusing on the needs as defined by the very people they exist to serve. Whether you design a local service delivery model or seek to modify a national model, the ultimate test is whether it fulfills the mission you have established based on clearly definable and quantifiable community needs.

The second question that your organization has to be cognizant of is, "Can our organization raise the necessary revenues to ensure that we can operate the service delivery model as designed based on meeting the needs of the community?" This is a key question that both Boards of Directors and professional staff have to address in a brutally honest manner. We have all seen organizations that are overly zealous in what they are trying to achieve only to fail and cease to exist when they could have chosen a more conservative model that, while not being as high profile, would have served fewer numbers in a more efficient manner and still deliver significant impact and outcomes. In most cases, having to decide whether you want to be the biggest or best always errs on the side of best. It is more important to try and help some people well than to try and help lots of people poorly, which can lead to collapse. Innovative thinking on the part of your staff and board can address the size of your service population, and how you serve them needs to be based on affordability and consistent service, not numbers. I have seen viable organizations get into trouble trying to grow too quickly

7

*Quality and Impactful
Services to Clients -
Begin with the End*

without a plan to develop the additional revenues needed to sustain the larger populations. One of my favorite sayings is, "If you try to be everything to everybody, you wind up being nothing to no one."

A third question that needs to be addressed is, "Do we have the necessary infrastructure to succeed?" This question relates not only to your facilities but to how and where you provide your services. Location of your services is a key element in answering this question as is the type of facilities you use and how you secure them. In many cases, nonprofit organizations see themselves as their own little empire. They want their own facilities, their own equipment, and to be answerable to no one but themselves. Take a lesson from the concept discussed earlier on collaboration and partnership; this is rapidly becoming the wrong approach. In most communities today, there are vacant buildings, municipal buildings, and schools that are only used part of the day, and a variety of other options other than building dedicated facilities. Collaborations and partnerships between diverse agencies that have different time constraints on their programs and services can actually occupy the same space at different times and share equipment as a cost-effective alternative to empire building. Senior citizen centers and after-school, youth-serving organizations can cohabitate in one facility, demonstrate cost effectiveness, and never conflict in their programming schedules. On the contrary, cross programming may actually become an option that enhances both programs while still demonstrating cost efficiency. The reality is that creative and innovative thinking applied by the staff and board can uncover facilities that not only enhance their programs and service delivery model but make it more affordable, which can be translated into helping more people and executing the mission more effectively.

The Perfect Example: Location! Location! Location!

We once conducted a feasibility study to determine the ability to raise money for a new organization. We were testing a campaign goal of five million dollars in a location that had been donated to the organization. When we analyzed the final results of the study, we found a very interesting result. The community-at-large indicated that the location of the property donated was not where the organization needed to be. As a result, they indicated they would not support the campaign and they felt it was doomed to fail. However, upon further questioning, it was discovered that there was almost unanimous agreement that the organization needed to build on the other side of town where the vast majority of their service population lived. These same people said they would support a campaign to build on this site wholeheartedly. The donated land was not taken and the organization secured a piece of property in the part of town designated in the study, which they had to pay for. The end result was that the community showed almost unanimous support for the campaign to build on the site they identified and the campaign was hugely successful, actually surpassing their goal.

Quality and Impactful Services to Clients - Begin with the End

A final question to be answered in designing your service delivery model is, "What are our plans for future growth?" Every nonprofit organization regardless of mission and focus wants to make a demonstrable impact in their community once they have proven themselves to continue to grow and serve greater numbers. The focal point here is the service delivery model you choose must be easily replicated in the future as you succeed and seek to serve greater numbers. Do your facilities pose a size limitation on future growth? Does the type of service you offer lend itself to other kinds of locations in your community? Someday do you wish to take your services to surrounding communities and become a more regional organization? These are all questions that must not only be anticipated but must be answerable as you design a new service delivery model or modify an existing one. These are simple questions that may in fact require complex answers. However, this reinforces the concept of whether you want your organization to be reactive or proactive. This simple concept of choosing to be reactive or proactive can be the single-most important aspect of your success or failure. It is critical that this be taken into consideration as you define your service delivery model and begin to implement it.

Summary

There are many factors that go into evaluating, defining, designing, and launching a service delivery model for your organization. Getting the right information on which to base your planning is critical. It is important to evaluate information and be responsive when questions arise. Ensuring that you are meeting the defined needs of your community can make all the difference in the world as to whether you succeed at the highest level or fail. Understanding the key questions that need to be answered provides you with the necessary infrastructure to be successful. Lastly, making a conscious decision to be proactive in developing your service delivery model and taking the necessary steps as outlined in this chapter set the table for ultimate success.

Evaluate your current mission, determine if you have the necessary information to decide whether you are meeting certifiable needs within the community, and ask yourself if you've used this information in developing or modifying your service delivery model. If you can truly say you have the necessary information and have done all of these things, you are the right road. If not you need to make the necessary adjustments to conform to this process or prepare to struggle and lose ground to your competition.

Further information, tools, and services are available at www.theperfectnonprofit.com

7

Quality and Impactful Services to Clients - Begin with the End

Diagnostic - Measuring your Perfection Quotient

Many readers of this book may be local member organizations of a large regional or national organization that, in return for dues paid, provides you with technical assistance. This varies from organization to organization. Also, as a part of that affiliation, you may be privy to a metric of some kind that measures your effectiveness. If you have a measurement tool like this already in place that gauges your effectiveness, congratulations because you are in the minority. If you do not, you will be introduced to a tool that will help you measure your effectiveness.

The diagnostic is aimed at measuring your organization's success and identifying its gaps in *The Perfect Nonprofit* Model. There is no underlying strategy or cause we are attempting to place upon you. The diagnostic tool we have developed will help you create a baseline where your organization falls in reference to *The Perfect Nonprofit* and what your Perfection Quotient is after completing the assessment.

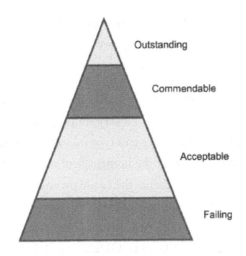

Outstanding

Commendable

Acceptable

Failing

*Diagnostic - Measuring
your Perfection
Quotient*

Grade Levels for the Perfection Quotient

As with any diagnostic or assessment tool, the work begins once you complete the assessment. We have developed tools and services that will help you move towards being *The Perfect Nonprofit*. The questions that are asked on the diagnostic tool are based on core beliefs that we have developed over our forty-five-plus years of working and consulting in the nonprofit sector. Once you complete the diagnostic, you will receive a Perfection Quotient report. The report will give your organization grades for its performance according to each of the Key Components of *The Perfect Nonprofit* Model as well as its overall Perfection Quotient. These grades are explained in the report together with your answers to each question and the ideal answers. This information indicates where your organization needs to focus its attention for improvement. All of this is based on *The Perfect Nonprofit* Model.

Another unique aspect of the diagnostic is its design. You can either take the diagnostic as an individual, or you can have several members of your organization complete the diagnostic and build consensus, which will result in a more comprehensive Perfection Quotient for you organization. The result of this is the creation of some rich dialogue that will allow you to see your organization as it is viewed by you and others as a whole. Imagine the possibilities this presents to you and your organization. This tool will prove to be the catalyst that will drive your organization to become a more Perfect Nonprofit.

So, if you are still interested, your next question is, "How do I take the diagnostic?" It is a very simple process. Simply click on your Internet browser and type in www.theperfectnonprofit. com. You will arrive at the homepage of our website. Follow the directions from there. The entire process is painless. As a matter of fact, it is quite engaging. All questions identified in the diagnostic are designed in multiple-choice format. The hard part is ANSWERING THE QUESTIONS HONESTLY in order to receive the correct Perfection Quotient score.

It is as simple as point and click. You will receive your individual perfection quotient score for your organization upon completion. As stated above, our hope is that you will have several of your key stakeholders in the organization complete the diagnostic as well. This will give you a much more complete and rich assessment plus a deeper look that equates to a more honest Perfection Quotient.

What a deal. You take the diagnostic and *The Perfect Nonprofit* website compiles your report so that you will be able to adapt easily and possibly take to a prospective donor to fund your organization's plan to build your capacity to do and serve more. It is just that simple.

We have taken the liberty to include the first run of the diagnostic quality statement and multiple-choice answers below. You must visit www.theperfectnoprofit.com to complete the assessment and receive your official Perfection Quotient. Good luck!

Perfection Quotient Quality Statements

Mission and Vision

1. The organization has core values that are not negotiable.

    a. The Board of Directors has core values developed by key senior staff.

    b. The organization has core values developed at a joint board/staff retreat.

    c. The organization has no specifically stated core values.

    d. The organization has core values developed by the Board of Directors.

2. The organization has a clearly defined Mission Statement.

    a. The organization has a mission that has not been evaluated for effectiveness in years.

    b. The organization has a mission statement that has been formally adopted by the current board.

    c. The organization has a clearly defined Mission Statement.

    d. The organization does not have a Mission Statement.

3. All key decisions of the organization are based on mission and vision.

    a. The organization makes all key decisions without referencing their impact on mission and vision.

    b. There is no formal process to reference mission and vision when making key decisions.

    c. The organization has a formal process to evaluate all key decisions against its mission and vision.

    d. All key decisions are made by the professional leadership without referencing impact on mission and vision.

4. The organization's Mission Statement is based on meeting the needs in the community.

   a. The organization has no Mission Statement.

   b. The organization's Mission Statement is historical and has no relationship to meeting current community needs.

   c. The organization's Mission Statement is based on actual needs that have been identified in the community.

   d. The organization's Mission Statement is based on perceived needs in the community.

5. The organization understands the concept of vision.

   a. The organization's leadership, both professional and volunteer, has a clear understanding of vision.

   b. The organization's senior staff clearly understands vision.

   c. The organization's Board of Directors clearly understands vision.

   d. No one in the organization understands the concept of vision.

6. The organization has a strategic plan that actively engages all stakeholders.

   a. The organization has a formal strategic plan.

   b. The organization has a formal strategic plan that identifies and engages all stakeholders.

   c. The organization does not identify or engage stakeholders.

   d. The organization does not have a formal strategic plan.

7. The organization has a long-range strategy for the future.

   a.   The organization has a long-range strategy but has no goals and objectives it ensure its success.

   b.   The organization has no long-range strategy.

   c.   The organization has a long-range written strategy but does not reference it in making decisions.

   d.   The organization has a long-range strategy for the future that guides it in making key decisions.

8. The organization's annual goals and objectives are aligned with the strategic plan.

   a.   The organization's annual goals and objectives have no relation to its strategic plan.

   b.   The organization's annual goals and objectives are in full alignment with the strategic plan.

   c.   The organization does not have a long strategic plan.

   d.   The organization does not have annual goals and objectives.

Professional Leadership

1. The Executive is capable and effective.

   a.   The Executive is qualified to hold the position and performs all tasks in an efficient and effective manner.

   b.   The Executive is efficient at most of the tasks of the job.

   c.   The Executive is not qualified for the position and has no understanding of the tasks of the job.

   d.   The Executive has most of the qualifications for the job and performs the tasks of the job at an acceptable level.

2. The Executive successfully carries out the strategic direction of the organization.

    a.   The Executive is aware of the strategic goals of the organization and works toward the successful completion of those goals.

    b.   The Executive is aware of the strategic goals of the organization, but only works toward those goals when they are in alignment with his priorities.

    c.   The Executive works in concert with the Board of Directors in assuring the organization has a well-established strategy in place to assure organizational effectiveness.

    d.   The Executive is not aware of any strategies set forth by the organization. He operates independently.

3. The Executive assures financial viability and transparency.

    a.   The Executive assures that all financial affairs of the organization are handled in an open and clear fashion.

    b.   The Executive handles all financial activity with little or no board input or oversight.

    c.   The Executive handles all finances of the organization and reports those activities to the board at regularly scheduled meetings.

    d.   The Executive works with the finance committee of the board to assure that all agency financial activities are legal, obvious, and understood by all stakeholders of the organization.

4. The Executive has a clear understanding of his roles and responsibilities in conjunction with the Board of Directors. There is a clear balance of power between the Executive and the Board of Directors.

a. The Executive and the board work in partnership to achieve organizational goals and objectives. Board members understand their role as well as understand the role of the Executive. In addition, the Executive clearly understands the role of the board, and his role in achieving the success of the organization.

b. The Executive and the board have conflict when attempting to understand the separation of powers of the organization.

c. The Executive and the board are constantly in conflict over organizational issues. There is no cohesiveness or any agreement on organizational goals and objectives.

d. The Executive includes the board on most of the activities of the organization. There is a clear line of separation between board activities and the Executive's responsibilities.

5. The Executive has a clear understanding of client needs and uses it to drive the organization.

a. The Executive and staff determine programs and services based on their knowledge of those programs and services.

b. Occasionally, the Executive visits with clients of the organization. The programs and services offered are determined by the staff with limited client and board input.

c. The executive is in constant communication with the clients of the organization. Surveys and questionnaires are developed to assure clients are receiving needed services and programs.

d. Programs and services of the organization remain the same and no organizational external surveys are conducted.

6. The Executive engages the board in and effective and creative manner.

    a.   The Executive regularly has individual meetings with board members to strategize about the affairs of the organization.

    b.   When needed, the executive will ask for board input to build organizational consensus.

    c.   The Executive asks for board input only when crisis is on the horizon.

    d.   The Executive has no relationship with the board.

7. The Executive has a formal process for recruitment, employment, and retention of staff.

    a.   The organization does have a formal application process, but the interview process and final decision for hiring of all positions rest with the Executive.

    b.   When hiring, the organization has an application process but no formal interviews with consistent questions or interview teams are conducted.

    c.   The organization has no strategy for the placement of the employees.

    d.   A formal process exists to identify, interview, and employ the best candidate possible for employment with the organization.

8. The Executive creates an organizational culture that promotes innovation and mutual respect.

    a.   The Executive allows employees to drive certain organizational strategies.

    b.   The Executive drives all organizational strategies while assigning certain tasks to other employees.

    c.   The Executive does not allow employee input or buy in

to organizational strategies.

  d. Employees are discouraged from taking on any extra
      responsibilities.

9. The Executive is a recognized leader in the community.

  a. The Executive is known by the people in the
      community.

  b. The Executive believes the organization operates
      effectively without community stakeholders.

  c. The Executive spends some time promoting the
      organization in the community.

  d. The Executive is looked upon as an expert in their field
      in the community.

Resource Development and Marketing

1. The organization has a resource development plan.

  a. The organization does resource planning but has no
      formal plan.

  b. The organization's resource development plan is a long-
      range plan with no annual objectives.

  c. The organization has a formal annual resource
      development plan.

  d. The organization does not have a resource development
      plan.

2. The organization has diversified revenue streams.

  a. The organization has diversified revenue streams with
      no one stream exceeding 30 percent of the total income
      budget.

  b. The organization has one revenue stream exceeding 50

percent.

c. The organization is totally dependent on one source of funding.

d. The organization does not evaluate its revenue budget by revenue stream.

3. The organization has diversified resource development strategies (i.e. Face-to-Face Asks, Special Events, etc.)

a. The organization is afraid to try new resource development strategies.

b. The organization uses a single focus to generate funding.

c. The organization has a diversified resource development strategy.

d. The organization uses one or two traditional fundraising strategies.

4. The organization has systematic processes for donor and volunteer development.

a. The organization has a formal process for developing new donors and volunteers.

b. The organization develops new donors as they are brought in by the board but has no formal process.

c. The organization relies on long-term donors and volunteers but does not actively seek new ones.

d. The organization only develops new donors when it is approached by the donor.

5. The organization raises sufficient funds to meet service objectives.

a. The organization does not raise sufficient funds to meet

service objectives.

b. The organization has no formal process to evaluate whether it is meeting it service objectives.

c. The organization raises sufficient funds to meet service objectives.

d. The organization often falls short in raising funds to meet its services objectives.

6. The organization has strong stewardship and cultivation programs.

a. The organization has strong stewardship and cultivation programs.

b. The organization does not have a strong stewardship or cultivation program.

c. The organization has a strong stewardship program but no cultivation program.

d. The organization has a strong cultivation program but no stewardship program.

7. The organization has systematic process for donor tracking and acknowledgment.

a. The organization does not have a systematic process for donor tracking and acknowledgement.

b. The organization has a systematic process for donor tracking.

c. The organization has a systematic process for donor tracking and acknowledgment.

d. The organization has a systematic process for stewardship.

8. The organization has a marketing plan.

a. The organization has a marketing plan.

b. The organization does not have a marketing plan.

c. The organization has a plan but does not use it.

d. The organization has a plan but it has not been updated or used for more than a year.

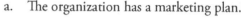

8

9. The organization has a well-recognized and positive brand.

a. The organization does not have a brand.

b. The organization has a brand but it is linked with multiple agencies.

c. The organization has a well-recognized and positive brand.

d. The organization does not have a well-recognized and positive brand.

10. The organization utilizes market research to determine marketing and resource development capacity.

a. The organization does not utilize market research.

b. The organization does not know how to use market research.

c. The organization utilizes market research to determine marketing and resource development capacity.

d. The organization's market research is limited to talking amongst the staff and board.

11. The organization has a targeted marketing strategy.

a. Organization has a targeted marketing strategy.

b. The organization does not have a targeted marketing strategy.

c. The organization is not aware of what a marketing

strategy entails.

d. The organization does not use marketing.

Board Leadership

1. The organization is proactive.

   a. Organizational decisions are made based on future needs not current problems.

   b. The organization assures current issues are addressed and resolved.

   c. The organization responds to issues after they occur.

   d. The organization is constantly reacting to its environment.

2. The board is a cohesive group made of volunteers representing all key constituencies of the community.

   a. The board is close from a social perspective, but lack in covering the key constituencies needed.

   b. The board has no influences with key constituencies and there is no social glue holding it together.

   c. The board is cohesive and represents all constituencies of the community.

   d. The board members fit this description, but there is little social glue holding them together.

3. The organization has a board contract with clearly defined expectations.

   a. Board members know the responsibilities but are not clear on the execution of those responsibilities.

   b. Board roles and responsibilities are identified but there is no document ensuring the successful execution of these responsibilities.

c.   Board members know their roles and responsibilities and understand how to carry out those responsibilities.

d.   There is no board contract.

4. The board sets the strategic direction of the organization.

a.   Board members know and can clearly articulate strategic goals and objectives of the organization.

b.   Board members know the mission of the organization but are unclear on the future of the organization.

c.   Board members are not aware of any clear strategic direction of the organization.

d.   The organization has no strategic direction.

5. The board assures adequate resources are garnered to meet the objectives of the organization.

a.   There is no board support for resource development.

b.   The board performs fundraising tasks, but there is no goal behind those efforts.

c.   The board has specific goals that individually and collectively assure the organization operates efficiently.

d.   The board supports the staff on occasion with the fundraising efforts of the organization.

6. All board members are giving an annual sacrificial gift.

a.   A few board members are making annual gifts.

b.   No board members give to the organization.

c.   Board members are only giving an annual gift but the gift is made in a sacrificial way.

d.   All board members are making annual gifts.

7. All board members are attending and actively participating in committee board meetings on a regular basis.

   a. The board has active committees and regular board meetings in which 70 percent of members are in attendance.

   b. The board has a committee structure but meetings are not regular or well attended. There are regular board meetings in which there are more than 50 percent in attendance.

   c. The board has regular board meetings in which there is more than 50 percent attendance. There is no committee structure.

   d. The organization holds board meetings on an as-needed basis and rarely do more than 50 percent of the members attend.

8. The board has a clear understanding of the roles and responsibilities and the balance of power between it and the agency executive.

   a. The board responds to the needs of the agency executive but there is no clear balance of powers or knowledge of roles and responsibilities.

   b. The board works closely with the agency executive while both parties understand their roles and responsibilities.

   c. The agency Executive operates independently of the board.

   d. The board operates independently of the Executive.

9. The board has an identification and recruitment strategy in place.

   a. There is a board recruitment strategy, but there is little

8

fault put toward diversity.

b. Members are recruited to the board on an annual basis.

c. There is no board recruitment process.

d. The board recruitment strategy is aimed at getting those who possess the skills needed to increase the expertise of the organization.

Governance

1. Bylaws have been amended to assure the organization operates legally.

a. The bylaws are up to date and are reviewed regularly by the Board of Directors and legal counsel.

b. The organization reviews bylaws occasionally.

c. It has been many years since bylaws were reviewed.

d. The organization does not have bylaws.

2. The organization operates within its bylaws and constitution.

a. The bylaws and constitution are considered before major decisions are taken.

b. The organization rarely consults its bylaws and constitution.

c. The organization consults its bylaws and constitution if someone thinks the decision may be affected by them.

d. The organization never consults its bylaws and constitution.

3. The organization knows and understands the legal duties of the Board of Directors

a. The legal duties of the Board of Directors are documented and each director and executive director have been oriented about them.

b. The legal duties of the Board of Directors are not documented but are known by each director and executive director.

c. We would call our lawyer if we thought we had a problem.

d. We have never discussed the legal duties of the Board of Directors.

4. The organization follows Generally Accepted Accounting Principles (GAAP) to ensure financial transparency.

a. We follow GAAP and this is overseen by an audit committee of the Board of Directors.

b. We follow GAAP.

c. We have a professional accountant (CPA) prepare our financial statements.

d. We have a bookkeeper prepare our financial statements.

5. The organization has strong ethics policies including conflict of interest and whistleblower protection policies.

a. We have some ethics policies but not all of them.

b. Our board and staff know what is right and wrong.

c. Our organization has documented ethics policies including conflict of interest and whistleblower protection policies. These are known by each board member and employee. Compliance with these is reviewed independently at least once a year.

d. Our organization has documented ethics policies including conflict of interest and whistleblower protection policies. These are known by each board member and employee. Compliance is self-assessed.

6. The organization has financial policies and procedures and

they are complied with.

    a.   Our organization has documented financial policies and procedures. Compliance with these is reviewed independently at least once a year by the audit committee of the Board of Directors.

    b.   Our organization has documented financial policies and procedures. The Board of Directors reviews financial statements every month.

    c.   The Executive Professional reviews the financial statements.

    d.   Our bookkeeper/accountant knows how to keep financial records and create financial statements.

7. The organization files all necessary legal documents in a timely and orderly fashion.

    a.   Filing dates and requirements are documented and scheduled. The Executive Professional reviews filings regularly.

    b.   The Executive Professional supervises the bookkeeper/accountant's work including filings.

    c.   Filing dates and requirements are documented and scheduled. Compliance with these is reviewed independently at least once a year by the audit committee of the Board of Directors.

    d.   Our bookkeeper/accountant knows what documents need filing and do so accordingly.

8. The organization has a record retention policy.

    a.   We have a documented record retention policy that is reviewed annually by legal counsel. Compliance with these is reviewed independently at least once a year by the audit committee of the Board of Directors.

b. We have a documented record retention policy. Compliance with these is reviewed by the Executive Professional.

c. We have a documented record retention policy but it has not been reviewed for three years or more.

d. Our bookkeeper/accountant knows what documents should be retained.

9. There is a well-defined committee structure within the organization.

a. The Board of Directors establishes committees and their responsibilities and objectives. Each committee is comprised of people who volunteer for membership.

b. We have had the same committee structure for many years.

c. The Board of Directors establishes committees. Each committee is comprised of people with appropriate experience.

d. We do not have committees. The Board of Directors works on everything.

10. Each committee has a meaningful purpose and is impactful.

a. The Board of Directors establishes committees and their responsibilities and objectives. Committees meet regularly and report on their work to the Board.

b. Our Board committees establish their own objectives. Committees meet regularly and report on their work to the Board.

c. Some committees do not function well. The effectiveness of each committee is dependent on the level of interest of its members.

d. We don't have committees. The Board of Directors

works on everything.

8

High Quality and Impactful Services to Clients

1. Programs and services delivered are valued by the community.

   a.   The community has no knowledge of the programs and services delivered by the organization.

   b.   The programs and services delivered by the organization are based on perceived needs in the community.

   c.   All of the programs and services delivered by the organization are valued by the community.

   d.   The organization does not take community needs into consideration when planning programs and services.

2. The organization shows due diligence in implementing programs and services.

   a.   The organization has a formal due diligence policy when implementing programs and services.

   b.   The organization does some due diligence but not in a formal policy.

   c.   The organization does not conduct due diligence when implementing programs and services.

   d.   Due diligence is done but is not used in implementing programs and services.

3. The organization has an objective means of measuring outcomes.

   a.   The organization does not measure outcomes.

   b.   The organization measures outcomes but has no formal objectives for doing so.

c. The organization has a formal process for measuring the outcomes of its programs and services.

d. Outcomes measured by the organization use no objective evaluation methods.

4. Programs and services meet client needs and generate positive outcomes.

a. The organization's programs and services meet client needs and generate positive outcomes.

b. The organization's programs and services meet client needs but outcomes are not measured.

c. The organization's programs and services do not meet current client needs.

d. The organization has no way to determine if its programs and services meet client needs or are generating outcomes.

5. The organization is constantly communicating with clients to affirm current and develop future services.

a. The organization communicates with clients but does not generate information relative to programming or services.

b. The organization does not consult clients when planning future programs.

c. The organization has no formal communications program to reach clients.

d. The organization has a formal means of communicating with clients to affirm current and develop future services.

6. The organization's programs and services meet its core

competencies.

    a. The organization knows its core competencies but does not measure its programs and services against them.

    b. The organization has no core competencies.

    c. The organization's programs and services meet its core competencies.

    d. The organization does not know its core competencies.

7. The organization looks to develop opportunities for collaborations and partnerships when appropriate.

    a. The organization is always looking for opportunities for collaboration and partnership.

    b. The organization has a formal process for exploring possible collaborations and partnerships.

    c. The organization is not interested in collaborations and partnerships.

    d. The organization might be interested in collaboration and/or partnership if approached but has no policy concerning such.

Further information, tools, and services are available at www.theperfectnonprofit.com

Perfect Practice Makes Perfect

We are at the point in the book in which we have completely explained *The Perfect Nonprofit* Model and the covenants that surround it. It simply comes down to this: we merely have theory versus application. If you do not pick up the book again after your first read, we have done you no good. We truly feel what we have laid forth in this book can move your organization to heights that you and your organization to this point would have never dreamed.

I had the pleasure recently to attend a training meeting organized by a national nonprofit. The presenter in his opening comments touched on the fact that organizations are in different mindsets at many different times. One thing is for sure: nonprofits and their organizational capacity are as diverse as diverse can be. This facilitator went on to add that in his experiences in visiting nonprofits, he would ask a very simple question, "How are things going?" He went on to explain that he would typically get two types of answers to the question. The first response would be gloom and doom. The response would be about how bad things were and how there was no real way to make things any better. The second response he would get would be one of hope. He would hear how things were getting better and about the new strategies the organization was contemplating for the future. In wrapping up his talk, he stated there was really only one difference in the organizations in which he visited. Expectations! One organization expected the best and the other expected the worst. What type of organization are you? Does this make a difference in your culture? Let me answer the question. Yes!

Herein lies the premise of the book. It is our hope that you will use this and the website as your organizational development tool. We firmly profess that if you and your organization focus on *The Perfect Nonprofit* Model and the belief that taking a holistic approach predicated by balance, you will make strides

9

toward the ultimate goal of the organization, the mission and vision.

The Perfect Nonprofit Model

Again, we cannot mention enough the ingredients that lead to success. As mentioned above, we believe that balance is essential to the long-term achievement of any nonprofit organization. Of course, we understand that your organization may have to focus its efforts on a particular area to gain balance. Professional leadership is essential to making this model run as we have outlined above. In addition, the organization must have a coordinated plan to market its brand and raise the dollars needed to achieve organizational goals and objectives. With this being said, board members play a key role in driving the organization to success. They must be engaged and committed to make this occur. Lastly, the organization must have a firm foundation from which to govern the organization. When these things happen, driven by the mission and vision of the organization, the clients being served will receive meaningful, deep services. As mentioned in the prologue of this book, this could truly create the "Perfect Game".

Getting Started

It is said that a journey begins with the first step. This is a very profound statement. You have completed the first step in moving your organization to greatness by reading this book. Your next step is to log on to www.theperfectnonprofit.com and complete the Perfection Quotient diagnostic. The diagnostic is free to complete.

Once you have completed the diagnostic you will get a comprehensive report that is specific to your organization. The diagnosis will be predicated on *The Perfect Nonprofit* model. In addition, comprehensive resources can be available to you on www.theperfectnonprofit.com.

Once you've completed these steps, your journey to organizational greatness will begin. It will be our honor to accompany you on this journey.

It is our vision and mission at Diversified Nonprofit Services and *The Perfect Nonprofit* for you to achieve greatness. It is that simple. In closing, we hope that you've enjoyed reading this book, that you will recommend it to others in the nonprofit sector, and that you will use it as your guide on your journey towards becoming *The Perfect Nonprofit*. We believe the best and most honorable people in the world either work at or volunteer for a nonprofit organization. Therefore, it has been our distinct honor to pour ourselves into this book.

Remember one thing: Perfect Practice Makes Perfect!

Further information, tools, and services are available at www.theperfectnonprofit.com

Glossary

Accountable

Having the responsibility to do something (e.g. a task). Accountability may be assigned based on a person's position description, delegated by someone in authority in the organization, or accepted voluntarily. Accountability may also be placed with a group such as the Board of Directors. Usually accompanied by expected standards of performance and timing.

Advisory Board

A group of people that the nonprofit assembles to provide expertise, guidance and recommendations. Sometimes used to engage people who have considerable experience or specialized knowledge but who may not wish to serve in a governance role.

See also Board of Directors; Corporator

Acknowledgement

Confirmation of the receipt of a donation or other value (e.g., volunteer time) and expression of thanks from the nonprofit.

Agency

A not-for-profit organization that has tax-free status.

Alternatives: Nonprofit, Charity, Charitable Organization; 501(c)(3); 501(c)(4); 501(c)(6)

Annual Campaign	A process through which the nonprofit raises money and other assets each year to support its programs, services and other operational costs.
Audit	Testing, analysis, verification and evaluation of financial statements.
	Also used to evaluate the effectiveness of processes within the nonprofit such as resource development.
Balance	Performing to a high standard in all of the areas defined by *The Perfect Nonprofit* Model: Mission and Vision; Board Leadership; Governance; Professional Leadership; Resource Development and Marketing; and High Quality and Impactful Services to Clients.
	See also Holistic
Bill of Rights, Donor	The Donor Bill of Rights ensures that philanthropy merits the respect and trust of the general public and donors and prospective donors can have full confidence in the nonprofits and causes they are asked to support.
	The Donor Bill of Rights was created by the Association of Fundraising Professionals (AFP), the Association for Healthcare Philanthropy (AHP), the Council for Advancement and Support of Education (CASE), and the Giving Institute.

Board of Directors	The governing body of the nonprofit. The primary responsibilities of the Board of Directors are to set policy and ensure the nonprofit has adequate resources. See also Corporator, Trustee
Board Chairperson	The Chief Volunteer Officer who leads the Board of Directors. Elected to this position by the Board of Directors according to its By-laws. Alternatives: Chief Volunteer Officer
Board Development	The process of creating and sustaining an effective Board. A Board Development process includes techniques for identification, cultivation, selection, recruitment, orientation, education, recognition, assessment, rotation, and separation of board volunteers.
Budget	The financial plan for income and expenses. Prepared for each fiscal year.
By-laws	The legal rules and regulations that are the framework for the operation of the nonprofit.
Campaign	A program to attract funds, volunteers, awareness or other assets to the nonprofit. See also Annual Campaign; Capital/ Endowment Campaign

Capacity, Organizational	The level of performance and effectiveness of a nonprofit. Includes the nonprofit's ability to perform in all areas defined by *The Perfect Nonprofit* Model. See also Balance; Holistic
Capacity to Give	The maximum level of donation which a person or organization is capable of making to a fund raising campaign.
Capital/ Endowment Campaign	A program to attract funds for buildings, equipment, infrastructure (capital) and to support programs/ services in perpetuity (endowment). See also Endowment
Charter	The legal document for the formation of the nonprofit. Alternative: Articles of Incorporation
Checks and Balances	The internal controls that safeguard assets, manage resources, ensure policies are implemented and ensure laws are complied with.
Client	The people and organizations served by the nonprofit. In a broad sense this includes those who use the programs/ services, the community, donors and volunteers. See also Customer

Collaboration　　Two or more organizations working together to meet needs in their community. Can be managed according to a legal agreement or informal. Can involve combined delivery of programs/services, shared assets (e.g., shared building space), shared fund raising campaigns, etc.

Alternative: Partnership

Community　　One or multiple groups of people who share a common identity (social, political and /or psychological unity among members of the community) based on location, ethnicity, race, religion, income level, age, lifestyle, political affiliation, interests, etc.

Community Assessment　　A Community Assessment is a study that uses objective information to evaluate the present state, and dynamics, of a community and their impact on your organization. It analyzes needs, identifies strengths and resources, and provides the information necessary to make informed decisions about programs and services.

Conflict of Interest	A situation where someone involved in making a decision or taking an action on behalf of the nonprofit has a personal interest that may, or may be perceived to, affect that person's decision about the situation to his/her own advantage.

Constituency Giving	Donations that are based on a person's affiliation with an organization or cause. Examples include church, university, or health related cause (e.g., donation to Heart Disease research by someone whose mother had a heart attack).
	Alternative: Affiliate Giving
Constitution	The By-laws and Charter that govern the operation of the nonprofit.
	See also: By-laws; Charter
Corporator	A member of the nonprofit. Volunteer structure. Part of a volunteer resource pool.
Cultivation	All the relationship building steps that lead to creating a tangible association between a potential donor and the nonprofit. Cultivation makes the solicitation possible; done well, it sets the stage for a successful "ask"

Customer	The people and organizations served by the nonprofit. In a broad sense this includes those who use the programs/services, the community, donors and volunteers.
	See also Client
Donation	Money or other asset given to a nonprofit by an individual or business.
	See also: Grant
	Alternative: Gift
Donor	A person or organization that gives money or other assets or in-kind services and/or products to the nonprofit.
	See also Investor
Duty of Care	Explicit or implicit responsibilities held by a person or persons towards others in the community or society.
Endowment	Money that is invested in perpetuity or for a defined period of time and which generates income that is used to support expenses of the nonprofit. The use of endowment income may be limited (restricted) to a defined use (e.g., a specific program/service) or may be used for any expenses of the nonprofit (unrestricted).

Executive Professional	The senior-most employee of the nonprofit. The Executive Professional is employed by, and reports to, the Board of Directors.

Alternative titles include Executive Director, Chief Professional Officer. |

Feasibility Study	A Feasibility Study uses objective information to evaluate the potential for success of a campaign (e.g., Capital/Endowment Campaign) or major project.
Focus Group	Focus groups are small groups, usually of 6 to 10 people, who take part in discussions about specific issues. The discussions are led by a facilitator who ensures that certain protocols are followed and all participants get to share their knowledge, experiences and opinions.
Foundation	A nonprofit organization that provides funding to other nonprofits in support of their programs/services or is the sole source of funding for its own programs/services.
Fund raising	The process by which a nonprofit secures financial support from donors.

Generally Accepted Accounting Principles / GAAP	Standards and rules that govern accounting and reporting by organizations, including nonprofits. GAAP are defined and administered by the American Institute of Certified Public Accountants (AICPA) and the Financial Accounting Standards Board (FASB).
Governance	The creation and implementation of policies by which the nonprofit meets the standards of trust and legal compliance expected by the public.
Grant	Funds given to a nonprofit by a foundation or government agency.
Grant Proposal	Formal request for funding from a foundation or government agency.
Holistic	The effectiveness of a nonprofit is not determined by its performance in each area of its operations but by to totality of its performance in the areas defined by *The Perfect Nonprofit* Model: Mission and Vision; Board Leadership; Governance; Professional Leadership; Resource Development and Marketing; and High Quality and Impactful Services to Clients.
	See also Balance

Impact	Measures of the total effect of programs/services that are provided by the nonprofit in mitigating the needs of the community.
	See also Need; Outcome
Investor	A donor who wants to know what results are achieved from the use of his/her donation. He/she considers his donation in similar terms to an investment in a for profit business although the returns expected are measured as benefits to the users of programs/services and improvements in the quality of life of the community.
	See also: Return on Investment
Market Research	Information gathered relative to the overall market (community), community needs and potential target markets.
	See also: Community Assessment; Feasibility Study; Focus Group
Marketing	The process of understanding customer needs and communicating with them.
Mission	Definition of the purpose of the nonprofit. Described in a Mission Statement.

Need   Description and quantification of deficiencies or challenges facing a segment of the community and the gap in programs/services to fill than need.

Nonprofit   A not-for-profit organization that has tax-exempt status.

Alternatives: Agency, Charity, Charitable Organization; 501(c)(3); 501(c)(4); 501(c)(6)

Outcome   Description and quantification of the results of a program/service when it is implemented by the nonprofit.

See also Impact

Perfect Nonprofit, The   A holistic approach to nonprofit management and leadership that focuses on balance. *The Perfect Nonprofit* Model is a guide for the professional and volunteer leadership of nonprofits that helps them make their organizations successful in meeting the needs and expectations of their constituents. *The Perfect Nonprofit* describes the characteristics of a proactive organization that is managed for long-term success.

Perfection Quotient   A holistic measure of a nonprofit's performance in all of the areas defined by *The Perfect Nonprofit* Model: Mission and Vision; Board Leadership; Governance; Professional Leadership; Resource Development and Marketing; and High Quality and Impactful Services to Clients.

See also: Balance; Holistic; Perfect Nonprofit

Planned Giving   Donations that are committed to be made on the occurrence of a specified event through instruments such as through wills, trusts and insurance policies.

Policy   The framework for decisions, actions, and performance established by the Board of Directors and implemented by the Executive Professional and his/her staff.

Positioning   The marketing process by which the nonprofit establishes its identity, products/services and image in the minds of its target market.

See also Marketing; Target Market

Process	The tasks and procedures that enable the nonprofit to achieve its goals, deliver programs/services to clients, safeguard and manage assets, and comply with laws and regulations.
Professional Staff	People with specific skill sets related to the mission that are employed by the nonprofit.
Program	An activity provided to benefit a person, group of people or community that requires involvement from the client. See also Services
Prospect	A potential donor or investor. See also Donor; Investor
Prospect Identification	The process of finding potential donors.
Prospect Rating	The process of evaluating philanthropic capacity of each prospective donor. See also Capacity to Give
Public Relations	A program that is directed at creating awareness, understanding and acceptance by the public.

Resource Development	The process of identifying and attracting resources needed by the nonprofit to attain its mission and meet its goals. It includes fund raising; human resources and leadership development; marketing and collaboration with other organizations.

Resource Development Audit	Analysis and evaluation of the resource development process and function.
Retention	The process of training, motivating, and rewarding professional staff and board members so that they continue to perform at a high level for the nonprofit. Can also relate to the retention of donors once they have a made a gift to your agency.
Return on Investment / ROI	The impact of programs/services expressed as a result of investment by donors. This is often qualitative and quantitative for donation to a nonprofit.
Sarbanes-Oxley	Oversight and reporting standards established for public companies. The philosophy (and some practices) of accountability and transparency have been adopted by leading nonprofits.

Also known as SOX; The Public Company Accounting Reform and Investor Protection Act |

Sequential Fund Raising	The process of stratifying prospective donors by their capacity to give and soliciting the highest level prospects first and then moving to the next level and so on.
Service	An activity provided to benefit a person, group of people or community that requires little or no effort from the client. See also Program
Service Delivery Model	The relationships of resources, programs/services and interactions with clients that result in the nonprofit attaining its mission. See also Programs; Services
Social Entrepreneur	A person who uses entrepreneurial practices to effect social change. As a minimum, social entrepreneurs look for a return on investment. Many become involved in the nonprofits they support with advice, direction, and other support. See also Return on Investment.
Solicitation	The act of asking a prospective donor to make a gift/investment of money or other assets or donate time/expertise to the nonprofit.

Special Event An event designed to attract donations to, and/or raise awareness of, the nonprofit.

Stewardship Stewardship is designed to assure the donor that he/she made a good decision in the giving to the nonprofit and to motivate the donor to continue with supporting the nonprofit. Stewardship involves using gifts in the manner in which they were intended, reporting to donors on the use of their gifts, then thanking, informing, and involving donors in the nonprofit.

Strategy A long-term plan to achieve a set of objectives and the allocation of resources to create value for the nonprofit and gain competitive advantage.

See also Tactic; Vision Statement

Strategy Development Strategy Development is a comprehensive planning process designed for nonprofits. The process creates strategies for the allocation of resources to create value for the nonprofit and gain a competitive advantage.

Tactic Steps (tasks) that move the nonprofit towards attainment of its strategies.

See also Strategy

Target Market	The group of people and organizations that the nonprofit wants to attract as customers. The nonprofit seeks to meet their needs through programs/services or by using their donations/support to make positive changes in the community.
	See also Customer.
Trustee	A senior member of the governance structure. Trustees provide financial support but rarely participate in the day to day governance of the organization as does the Board of Directors.
	See also Board of Directors
Vision	Definition of the envisioned future of the nonprofit. Establishes what the nonprofit will look like in the long-term. Described in a Vision Statement.
Volunteer	A person who donates his/her time and expertise to help to nonprofit.